GREAT ART TREASURES IN AMERICAN MUSEUMS

Great Art Treasures

IN AMERICAN MUSEUMS

BY THE EDITORS OF COUNTRY BEAUTIFUL

Editorial Direction: Michael P. Dineen •
Edited by Robert L. Polley • Text by
Harold Haydon, *Associate Professor of Art
and Director of the Midway Studios,
University of Chicago*

Published by COUNTRY BEAUTIFUL CORPORATION, Waukesha, Wisconsin 53186

COUNTRY BEAUTIFUL: *Publisher and Editorial Director:* Michael P. Dineen; *Executive Editor:* Robert L. Polley; *Managing Editor:* Charles R. Fowler; *Senior Editors:* Kenneth L. Schmitz, James H. Robb; *Associate Art Director (Design):* Pricilla Unverzagt; *Associate Art Director (Production):* William M. Dichtl; *Associate Editor:* Dorothy Hennessy; *Director of Marketing:* Mel Rozier; *Production Director:* John Dineen; *Administrative Assistant:* Sharon G. Armao; *Finance Assistant:* Trudy Schnittka; *Marketing Assistant:* Kathleen Kons; *Production Secretary:* Marlene Yogerst; *Editorial Secretary:* Gayle Butzek; *Distribution Director:* Arthur Meuler; *Production Assistant:* Lynn Simonson.

Country Beautiful Corporation is a wholly owned subsidiary of Flick-Reedy Corporation: President: Frank Flick; Vice President and General Manager: Michael P. Dineen; Treasurer and Secretary: August Caamano.

Left title page: MADONNA AND CHILD by a follower of Botticelli (16th century). Wood. This type of Madonna reflects Botticelli's late period and the mystically religious sculptures of Donatello. It appealed to artists trained in Botticelli's studio and there are a number of variants of the composition. It is difficult to determine how much of the work was done by the master and how much by his assistants. *El Paso Museum of Art,* El Paso, Texas. Samuel H. Kress Collection.

Right title page: PORTRAIT SCULPTURE OF QUEEN AMENIRDAS I. Egypt (c. 700 B.C.). Granite. Queen Amenirdas I was the sister of the Kushite King Piankhi who conquered Egypt in 716-715 B.C. Three-dimensional figures portraying her are quite rare. *Joslyn Art Museum,* Omaha, Nebraska.

Contents

Introduction

Two things should be said at once about the great art treasures in America's smaller museums: First, the museums are not always small by the standards of even a decade past, and they refuse to stay small; second, aggressive acquisition programs assure that the treasures of today will be augmented significantly tomorrow, just as new buildings are being planned almost before the first ones have settled.

In communities everywhere there are groups and individuals committed to enhancing the cultural life of the public by enlarging the opportunities for the enjoyment of art. This urge to share the experiences of art with others is not new, for it caused men and women to found some of the earliest museums. However, there are many more people interested today, and what once depended upon persons of great wealth is now frequently undertaken collectively by community organizations and local governments.

One consequence is the broad distribution of princely works of art among the smaller museums of America. A chief joy for the museum visitor can be the discovery of these hundreds of masterpieces, not only in the long-established institutions where one might expect to find them, but in recently established museums as well.

An example of the former is the superb Isabella Stewart Gardner Museum in Boston, which owns such treasures as "The Concert" by Jan Vermeer, "The Rape of Europa" by Titian, Carlo Crivelli's "St. George and the Dragon," Raphael's portrait of "Count Tommaso Inghirami" and equally famous works by Benvenuto Cellini, Rembrandt van Rijn and Peter Paul Rubens. One of the best of the newer museums is the Sterling and Francine Clark Art Institute in Williamstown, Massachusetts, which possesses "At the Concert," "The Ingenue" and "Bather Arranging Her Hair" among its fine collection of 30 paintings by Pierre Auguste Renoir.

Often as not, works which have been valued for centuries are in the collection of the same museum which owns pieces by esteemed modern artists. At the Joslyn Art Museum in Omaha, Nebraska, Titian's "Man with a Falcon" coexists with Sir Jacob Epstein's bronze bust, "Laughing Girl," while the fixed color harmonies of "Two Girls at a Piano" by Renoir may be compared with the shifting, dancing colors of Thomas Wilfred's composition, "Lumia — Space-Time Study, Opus 135."

Many of the museums have strong holdings in certain areas. The Walker Art Center in Minneapolis, for example, which emphasizes 20th-century art, shows Franz Marc's immortal "Blue Horses" and major pieces of sculpture — including "Reclining Mother and Child" by Henry Moore; "Cubi IX," a nine-foot-tall stainless steel work by David Smith; and Jacques Lipchitz's "Prometheus Strangling the Vulture."

Still another vein of special interest for Americans are those pictures and sculptures which are the result of the artists' discovery of the West. Among the most spectacular of these are the oils and watercolors by George Catlin recording his pioneer expedition up the Missouri in 1832; the panoramic views of the Rocky Mountains painted by Thomas Moran, Albert Bierstadt and others; and the eye-witness, picture-stories of frontier life when the West was wild, drawn, modeled and painted by Frederic Remington and Charles M. Russell. These important works are to be found in museums which concentrate on the art of the West, such as the Thomas Gilcrease Institute of American History and Art in Tulsa, Oklahoma, and the Whitney Gallery of Western Art in Cody, Wyoming, as well as several other institutions.

Sometimes it seems that there cannot be enough paintings and sculptures to go around among the galleries and museums, for they increase in absolute number at a formidable rate while most of them seek to expand and diversify their collections.

In truth, there are not enough of certain artists' works. Some collections may be forever incomplete, but the spectacular art possessions of European royalty and splendid hereditary collections still exist and can be tempted into the marketplace.

There was a time when a willingness to buy virtually called into being the works most highly prized, including spurious offerings eagerly accepted by collectors blinded by their desire to possess. One would be wrong to suppose that the days of trickery and fraud are entirely past, yet new attitudes of caution and critical evaluation have grown up in a century that prefers truth in art, and likes its masterpieces in as nearly original condition as possible. In many of the smaller museums a new breed of better trained curators and directors is clearing house and setting things in order little by little, with university-connected institutions tending to set the pace.

The search for truth is never-ending and must be pursued, yet enjoyment of the work of art need not be dulled by doubt and worries over attribution and authenticity. One can feel that a beautiful little panel painting is what it is no matter whose name and reputation is linked with it.

Practically all American museums began their collections too late to be able to acquire examples of the best medieval and Renaissance art, although even here one must note that occasionally very choice plums are acquired at previously unimaginable prices. To provide a beginning for the study of Western art, the Samuel H. Kress Foundation has supplied a number of museums with works that date from the 14th to the 18th centuries, chiefly Italian but with some northern European paintings and sculptures included. Simultaneously with starting a collection, or introducing a substantial new element into an existing collection, the Kress Foundation invariably laid down conditions for the housing and display of a Kress Collection that set standards for the museum and stimulated further growth — an important additional contribution.

There may be some questions, however, about the wisdom of a policy of acquiring a sample of everything on world-wide, ancient-to-modern scale. Although the ideal may be admired, the undertaking is enormous, and the few museums that have set out to be universal cannot expect to acquire prime examples in all areas. There is no question, however, about the value of the collections of Oriental, pre-Columbian, African and Oceanic art that broaden the experience of the arts for visitors to some fortunate museums.

A most interesting development is the specialized museum, for it may indicate a certain maturity in the art of collecting art. It was a magnificent advance to recognize that great and important art might be the art of Africa, of pre-Columbian America, of the American Indian, of the old West, or even of a single artist. In such museums single facets of the precious diamond of art may be enjoyed and studied in depth.

And why not let enjoyment be the primary aim and in itself enough? Each of the museums has its own interesting history and character, each undertakes to serve its community in many different ways. When the museum is a state institution it may even become a peripatetic teacher-on-wheels, taking the museum to the people in all parts of its territory. Libraries, lectures, classes and schools are only some of the extended activities related to the appreciation and experience of art that are centered in the museums. Furthermore, the idea of the art center, with its alliance and physical association of museum and the performing arts, makes it possible for the enjoyment of art to have many houses all together. From such conjunctions of the devotees of the several arts should come expanding audiences for each.

The accounts that follow will serve their purpose if the characterization of each museum, with reproductions and descriptions of some chief glories of its collections, provide the reader and the museum visitor with the means to that most important end — enjoyment.

— Harold Haydon

I NEW ENGLAND

ADDISON GALLERY
OF AMERICAN ART

When the Phillips Academy was founded in 1778, its stated purpose was to teach "the great end and real business of living." It was to further this aim that the distinguished Addison Gallery of American Art was established in 1930 by a gift from Thomas Cochran, an alumnus who preferred to remain anonymous at the time.

The painter Samuel F. B. Morse, an earlier graduate of Phillips Academy, would have approved of his fellow alumnus' limitation of the permanent collection to American art, although loan exhibits may come from any nation. Morse suffered from the Republic's neglect of art in his day, and, forced to abandon a brilliant beginning as an artist, he became the inventor of the telegraph. His "Self-Portrait" is in the Addison Gallery.

Truly living up to its name, the gallery holdings range from works by John Smibert, Benjamin West, Gilbert Stuart, Washington Allston and John Singleton Copley, to those by contemporary artists.

Among nearly 2,000 items, there are some charming pieces by unknown artists and craftsmen that make the life of an earlier America vividly tangible. Such are the running horse weathervane from Pennsylvania; the bucolic scene of pastoral employment, clearing, plowing and milking, inscribed "He that by the plough would thrive, Himself must either hold or drive"; and the recently acquired 1763 woolen coverlet with floral design.

The overpowering influence of the American environment which gave rise to the Hudson River School can be seen in paintings by Thomas Doughty, Asher B. Durand, Frederick E. Church, and their successors, George Inness, Alexander H. Wyant and Homer Martin. A group of Albert P. Ryder's moonlight mysteries are from this same period.

The flavor of the nearly extinct one-room school house can be sensed in Winslow Homer's oil, "New England Country School," the school marm hearing one of her classes in the sparsely populated room. A number of oils, including one of his finest, "Eight Bells" (p. 14), and watercolors by Homer make an important representation of his art.

Homer (1836-1910), one of the best American marine and landscape painters, liked to say, "When I have selected the thing carefully, I paint it exactly as it appears," and, at first glance, "Eight Bells" seems to depict its subject with the accuracy of a photograph. But closer examination shows that Homer has molded the literal image — by causing the shrouds at the right edge to dissolve upward and bathing much of the scene with brilliant moonlight — for dramatic emphasis. As Bartlett H. Hayes, Jr., Director of the Addison Gallery, has stated, "Just as a writer concentrates on a single character or event, the artist has singled out the two fishermen with optical clarity and subordinated other truths about the scene."

At 19, Homer became a commercial photographer's apprentice and shortly thereafter a free-lance illustrator. During the Civil War he became an illustrator-correspondent for *Harper's Weekly*. In his thirties, as he began to sell some oils and watercolors, the small, slight Homer became a taciturn individual. He even put a sign reading, "Coal Bin," on his studio door to keep people out. At 48, he retired to Prout's Neck on the Maine coast where he painted "Eight Bells," a superb example of his profound but clear vision, deliberate nature and firm hand.

In addition to fine portraits by Thomas Eakins, the Addison Gallery owns his "Salutat" in which the young fighter, stripped to the buff and followed by his seconds, is shown accepting applause from the crowd. The expatriates, Mary Cassatt, James A. McNeill Whistler and others under the spell of European training, round out the 19th century.

The gallery generously documents how American painting of the 20th century sounded a new call to romantic realism in the work of "The Eight" of the Ashcan School, among them Robert Henri, John Sloan, William Glackens and George Luks. Sloan, who used to gaze out over the rooftops of New York from his studio window, caught a bit of apartment dwellers' "high life" in "Sunday, Women Drying Their Hair" on the roof, as Luks captured the spirit of childhood in "The Spielers" on the street.

Such American scene painters of the depression

(Continued on page 15)

New England Museums

Left: THE BALLET DANCER DRESSED. Bronze. Courtesy of the *Sterling and Francine Clark Art Institute,* Williamstown, Massachusetts. Below: THE TUB. Pastel. *The Hill-Stead Museum.* Both by Edgar Degas (1834-1917). In later years, his sight failing rapidly, Degas turned to less demanding media, creating fine bronzes, and, in pastel, combining truly superlative design and luminescence to transcend what was often the awkward realism of his subjects.

Left: ST. GEORGE AND THE DRAGON by Carlo Crivelli (c. 1440-c. 1493). Tempera on wood. Detailed and fanciful, this 15th-century Venetian composition was probably part of a large Adriatic cathedral altarpiece. *Isabella Stewart Gardner Museum*.

Below: ECCE HOMO by Andrea da Solario (c.1460-c. 1522). Panel. This mystical and poetic study shows the influence of Leonardo da Vinci upon the artist's religious works. Courtesy of the *Sterling and Francine Clark Art Institute*, Williamstown, Massachusetts.

Left: THE WARRIOR by Jean Fragonard (1732-1806). Oil. The artist's Portraits of Fantasy, exemplified by the arrogant, unstable and dictatorial visage of The Warrior, were revealing character studies of different kinds of people. Courtesy of the *Sterling and Francine Clark Art Institute,* Williamstown, Massachusetts.

Below: LANDSCAPE WITH OBELISK by Rembrandt van Rijn (1606-1669). Etching. In every genre, the quality and variety of this Dutch master's work is unparalleled in its excellence. *Isabella Stewart Gardner Museum.*

Above: HEPTAPTYCH by Ugolino da Siena (Active c. 1317-c. 1339). Wood panels. This exceedingly well-preserved altarpiece, complete save for its frame, is both subtle and opulent in the true Byzantine tradition and style, which Ugolino invariably preferred. Courtesy of the *Sterling and Francine Clark Art Institute,* Williamstown, Massachusetts.

Below: EIGHT BELLS by Winslow Homer (1836-1910). Oil. With dramatic emphasis Homer symbolizes man plotting his course through the uncertainties of nature. *Addison Gallery of American Art,* Phillips Academy, Andover, Massachusetts.

(Continued from page 10)

years as Reginald Marsh, John Steuart Curry and Thomas Hart Benton continue the remarkably complete survey provided by the Addison Gallery, which extends into the present with works by Laszlo Moholy-Nagy, Jackson Pollock, Hans Hofmann, Andrew Wyeth, Alexander Calder, Richard Lippold and still younger artists whose names are not yet so well known. While constantly adding recent examples of American art, the gallery's acquisition policy also brings in significant pieces from earlier periods.

Some select examples of 18th-century American silver, colonial furnishings and models of famous American sailing ships, built to a uniform scale, are on permanent exhibition. American sculpture, thus far not extensively represented, is being augmented, as is the collection of photography.

Addison Gallery of American Art: Phillips Academy, Andover, Mass. Open daily, 9 a.m. to 5 p.m.; Sunday, 2:30 p.m. to 5 p.m. July and August: open daily, 11 a.m. to 5 p.m.; Sunday, 2:30 p.m. to 5 p.m.

Above: SALUTAT by Thomas Eakins (1844-1916). Oil. Eakins' stark realism was influenced by Spanish masters. *Addison Gallery of American Art*, Phillips Academy, Andover, Mass.

Above: THE SPIELERS by George Luks (1837-1933). Oil. Luks was a constant anathema to the academic art world because of his forthright portraits and studies. *Addison Gallery of American Art*, Phillips Academy, Andover, Massachusetts.

Above: Wool Coverlet. Connecticut Valley (1763). *Addison Gallery of American Art*, Phillips Academy, Andover, Mass.

HILL-STEAD MUSEUM

It is a typically generous American gesture for a collector of art who has assembled paintings and sculpture for his own pleasure to leave his collection to his neighbors for the enjoyment of succeeding generations rather than to sell or give it to one of the great museums. Although at his death in 1913 Alfred Atmore Pope had made no provision for the care of his small but exceptional collection, and a few pictures were sold after they descended to his daughter, Mrs. John Wallace Riddle, she soon determined to make the main part of his acquisitions a memorial to her father.

The collection survived during her lifetime in Hill-Stead, the neo-classical mansion on a hill in Farmington, Connecticut, that was described as "a magnified Mount Vernon" by Henry James when he wrote of Farmington in *The American Scene*. The structure was built for Pope by the famous architect Stanford White with "the zealous cooperation" of Pope's daughter, who selected the site and influenced her father to return to New England and Farmington after he had amassed a fortune with his Cleveland Malleable Iron Company.

The pictures he had collected, beginning as soon as he could afford them, remained in the unaltered turn-of-the-century house until Mrs. Riddle's death in 1946. By her will the house and all its contents were left in trust, the executors having been instructed to "maintain the same forever as a museum."

In the setting perpetuated from another age, the timeless paintings of Edgar Degas, Edouard Manet, Claude Monet, Mary Cassatt and James A. McNeill Whistler, among the leading artists of the day when Alfred Pope formed his collection, express his forward outlook in rooms and halls that reflect the quiet good taste of this son of a New England Quaker family.

Over the drawing room fireplace hangs Monet's "View of Bay and Maritime Alps in Antibes," bought in 1889, a purchase thought to have marked the beginning of the Pope collection. On either side are fine works by Degas (1834-1917). One is an arresting pastel called "The Tub" (p. 11), done in 1885, showing a nude model in a typical awkwardly graceful pose, the figure and appurtenances of the room asymmetrically composed, with a sensitive side lighting of the forms. This is perhaps the outstanding piece in the collection and, purchased in 1907, was the last to be acquired, for Pope was an unusual collector in that he called a halt when

Below: BOATS LEAVING THE HARBOR by Claude Monet (1840-1926). Oil. This youthful work by Monet recalls the scenes of his boyhood in Le Havre, and is a tribute to his first teacher, Eugène Boudin. Dramatic contrasts in tonality, flickering brushwork, and a concern for the effects of light and atmosphere forecasted the brilliance of the novice painter. *Hill-Stead Museum.*

he had filled the walls of his house.

Driven to seek a medium less demanding than oil paint, when his always poor eyesight began seriously to fail, Degas converted the minor art of pastel into one of consummate virtuosity. But his method in "The Tub" remained thoroughly traditional, as if to show that, by the meticulous blending of chalks over a layer of gouache, he could produce the illusion of a major work in oils; and the result here yielded a matchless drawing of the human figure and an example of superlative design and luminous atmosphere which transformed the subject into poetry. It has been suggested that Degas found in the repertoire of Michelangelo many of the calisthenic postures which he so deftly rendered, and which must have been so tiresome for the model. Whatever the source of his inspiration, Degas, a cantankerous bachelor, made his own use of it, changing mythological goddesses into mortal women and evoking from their homely postures domestic scenes of uncanny fidelity.

Other Degas works in the museum are the "Dancers," a painting of several members of the corps de ballet standing in the wings, and "Jockeys," a pastel depicting jockeys and their mounts exercising before the race. The collection holds three more paintings by Monet, two of his famed "Haystacks" and the early "Boats Leaving the Harbor." Manet is represented by a wash drawing of "The Absinthe Drinker"; "La Posada," a vivid painting of a troupe of Spanish dancers; and "The Guitar Player" in which his favorite model, Victorine Meurend, is dressed in white while playing the guitar. It was she who modeled for the nude figures in "Olympia" and "Luncheon on the Grass," both now in the Louvre but considered scandalous when first shown.

Of three paintings by Whistler, "The Blue Wave" of 1862 is an early work in solid realist manner, while the other two, a marine called "Symphony in Violet and Blue" and "Portrait of Carmen Rossi," are in the atmospheric and tonal manner for which the artist is chiefly known. A fine painting by Mary Cassatt, "Mother and Two Children," and one of her color etchings offer further proof that Alfred Pope was one of the most perceptive collectors of his time.

Among the prints are ten etchings by Whistler, two drypoints by Seymour Haden, early impressions of three Albrecht Dürer engravings, scenes of Paris by Charles Meryon and views of Rome by Giovanni Battista Piranesi, plus one signed etching by Henri Matisse. Japanese prints by Utamaro, Hiroshige, Hokusai and Harunobu are concentrated in Mrs. Pope's sitting room, while throughout the house in rooms and halls are examples of fine furniture, sculpture and porcelain.

Above: THE ABSINTHE DRINKER by Edouard Manet (1832-1883). Wash drawing. Like Degas, Manet translated the Parisian life of his time into a rich language of form and color, and received both fame and vilification. *Hill-Stead Museum.*

Viewed as a whole, this private collection, now available to the public, is both a monument to Alfred Atmore Pope and a testimonial to the taste and good judgment of a businessman who found in art, satisfactions to complement his business success.

Hill-Stead Museum: Farmington, Connecticut. Open Wednesday, Thursday, Saturday and Sunday, 2 p.m. to 5 p.m. Closed Thanksgiving and Christmas.

ISABELLA STEWART GARDNER MUSEUM

The Isabella Stewart Gardner Museum in Boston is among the finest art museums in the land. When it first opened its doors to an astonished public on February 23, 1903, the astonishment was twofold because of the sumptuous building reminiscent of a Venetian palace, with its central court of statues, fountains and blooming flowers, and because of the magnificence of the art collection for which the building was designed.

Casually arranged throughout the varied rooms, intermingled regardless of period with fine furnishings in the congenial and intimate atmosphere of a great house, were some of the world's finest masterpieces of painting and sculpture. They remain there now, left in trust, and by the will of a truly fascinating and remarkable art collector, Isabella Stewart Gardner, for the education and enjoyment of the public forever.

Below: The Dutch Room of the Isabella Stewart Gardner Museum typifies the combination of fine paintings and furnishings to be found throughout the former Gardner home. Over doorway: painted wood statue of "St. George and the Beggar." Paintings from left to right: "Portrait of the Artist as a Young Man" by Rembrandt van Rijn, "Portrait" by Albrecht Dürer and "Lady with a Rose" by Sir Anthony van Dyck. Center: 17th-century Dutch carved oak cabinet.

The creator of this magnificent collection married the eminently respectable John Lowell "Jack" Gardner when she was 20 years old; both families were well-to-do. Mrs. Gardner, who came to be known as "Mrs. Jack," was attractive without being beautiful; she inspired devotion, as well as envy; she had an agile, curious mind and a sense of drama. All of these qualities, along with a generous income, contributed to her success as an art collector.

The first sign of the collection could be seen by about 1890. She had met Bernard Berenson, who was to become a renowned art authority, while he was a student at Harvard in the mid-1880's. When the Gardners were in Europe in 1886 they met the American artists James A. McNeill Whistler and John Singer Sargent. Influenced by these acquaintances, in 1888, while Mrs. Gardner was in Seville, she bought a Francisco de Zurbarán Madonna.

Upon entering the museum, if one turns left into the Yellow Room there are to be seen two paintings by Whistler, "Nocturne, Blue and Silver: Battersea Reach," and an earlier work, "Harmony in Blue and Silver: Trouville." If, instead, one goes directly ahead to the Spanish Cloister, there in an alcove at the far end of the gallery he will find Sargent's rich and lively "El Jaleo," named for the Andalusian dance it depicts. Although painted in 1882 when the artist was 26, the great painting did not enter the Gardner collection until 1914, as a gift from her husband's relative, the Honorable T. Jefferson Coolidge, who bought it in 1887. Sargent also painted the full-length portrait of Mrs. Gardner that hangs in the third-floor Gothic Room.

It is singularly appropriate that among the first works of art encountered in the Gardner Museum one finds pictures by the two American painters who were, after a fashion, godfathers of the museum. Following their 1886 meeting, Mrs. Gardner became a patron of the young Whistler and Sargent.

After the Zurbarán, other works were bought, and then in 1892, at a Paris auction, Mrs. Gardner bid in "The Concert" by Jan Vermeer, one of the relatively few paintings known from the hand of this superb organizer of interior space. It came from the collection of Théophile Thoré Bürger who compiled the first history of Vermeer's art and had much to do with bringing attention to a long-neglected master.

The Gardner collection grew in stature with the wise counsel over the years of that other young friend, Mr. Berenson, who had quickly made himself a leading authority on Italian art. In 1894 he learned that Sandro Botticelli's "The Tragedy of Lucretia" might be for sale and, perhaps in gratitude for Mrs. Gardner's financing of his first European researches, he informed her of the opportunity which she promptly seized. Thereafter,

Berenson was instrumental in bringing many of the chief masterpieces into the collection.

When John Lowell Gardner died in 1898 after a distinguished career in business and civic affairs, the Gardners' notable holdings included, among others, Rembrandt van Rijn's "Self-Portrait at the Age of 23"; Titian's "The Rape of Europa"; the "Portrait of Philip IV" attributed to Velásquez as a copy of his Madrid painting; Sir Anthony van Dyck's portrait of a "Lady with a Rose"; Carlo Crivelli's "St. George and the Dragon"; the bronze bust of "Bindo Altoviti" by Benvenuto Cellini; and Peter Paul Rubens' portrait of "Thomas Howard, Earl of Arundel."

The first idea of a museum with a home in the upper floors dates back to 1896 when Mrs. Gardner asked the Boston architect William T. Sears to draw up some plans and pledged him to deepest secrecy. Following her husband's death, she moved swiftly to realize her dream, buying land in the Fenway as he had counseled, and proceeding with the construction without public explanation of her intentions. Not only did she raid Europe for architectural details to grace the build-ing, such as columns, capitals, ironwork, staircases, fountains, arches, gates and fireplaces, but she found time to search out paintings, sculpture, tapestries and other *objets d'art*, to add to the collection. Ultimately, at the time of her death in 1924, it numbered around 2,000 pieces, including 290 paintings and 280 sculptures.

Her life-long love of Italy inclined Mrs. Gardner's collection to Italian art. Yet Spanish and northern European art is significantly represented, and there are a few pieces from more distant lands. A granite "Hawk of Horus" in the court is from 4th-century B.C. Egypt; 17th-century wall tiles in the Spanish Cloister are from a ruined church in Mexico; in the Chinese Loggia is an 11th-century wooden "Kuan-yin," Deity of Compassion, from the Sung Dynasty; and a stone Buddha is in high relief on a "Vitive Stele" dated 543 A.D. There are 18th-century Japanese screens, a pair of very early "Bronze Bears," probably of the Han period, some Chinese paintings, and a miscellany of minor arts.

The Dutch Room holds four paintings and an etching by Rembrandt (1606-1669). In addition to the

Below: EL JALEO by John Singer Sargent (1856-1925). Oil. Sargent was 26 when he painted this intense and vibrant work. Based on drawings that he had made in Spain three years earlier, it was named after an Andalusian dance. Mrs. Gardner acquired the work in 1914 and later Sargent presented her with several preliminary sketches. *Isabella Stewart Gardner Museum.*

Above: MRS. GARDNER by John Singer Sargent (1856-1925). Oil. "Mrs. Jack," as John Lowell Gardner's wife came to be known, was 48 when the artist painted her wearing her famous pearls in three ropes, from each of which hangs a large ruby. She has been quoted as saying that this was the ninth attempt at the portrait and she considered it Sargent's finest portrait. The friendship between artist and subject which came about during the painting was to last throughout their lives. *Isabella Stewart Gardner Museum.*

self-portrait, there is the distinguished early double-portrait, "A Lady and Gentleman in Black," dating from 1633 when Rembrandt was 27 years old and a successful portraitist. His "Landscape with Obelisk" (p. 13) of 1638 displays a magnificent tension between the obelisk, the distant mountain and the wild cluster of trees, the branches of which, on the left, look like the arms of a ghost groping toward the center. The contrast between the dark foreground and highlighted middle distance also adds to the tempestuous mood and sweep of nature in which the figures in the foreground are hardly noticeable. An obelisk like this once stood about two miles from Amsterdam, but the remainder of the scene is different.

Works by Rubens, Jan Gossaert (called Mabuse), Vermeer, van Dyck, Frans Pourbus the Younger, Gerard ter Borch, Antonio Moro, and by two Germans, Albrecht Dürer and Hans Holbein the Younger, make an impressive assembly in this room. Dürer's "Portrait" is dated 1521, while Holbein's paintings are portraits, done in the last year of his life, of the scholar and physician, Sir William Butts, and Lady Butts.

Fine as many of these pictures are, the Italian representation is even more imposing. In the Room of Early Italian Paintings are five panels by Simone Mantini, a pentaptych of the "Madonna and Child with Saints Paul, Lucy, Catherine and John the Baptist," from the first quarter of the 14th century. The delightfully delicate yet colorful "Death and Assumption of the Virgin" by Fra Angelico (c. 1386-1455) is a tripartite treatment of the theme. In the lowest portion the Virgin is recumbent, surrounded by the Apostles with Christ in the center, holding in His arms a small child symbolic of the Virgin's Soul. The larger central portion portrays the slim and graceful figure of the Virgin lifted up to Heaven, surrounded by a celestial choir of youthful angels playing musical instruments. From the uppermost section of the painting the Deity leans forward with arms outstretched to receive the Virgin into Heaven.

The same room contains a fresco of the club-wielding "Hercules," from the house of the artist, Piero della Francesca. Dated before 1466, this work was on its original wall until 1903, entering the Gardner collection in 1906 through the hands of a dealer. Other paintings include Andrea Mantegna's "Santa Conversazione" and "Young Man in a Scarlet Turban" by Masaccio. Upstairs, in the Gothic Room, is Giotto's "Presentation of the Child Jesus in the Temple," a panel painting in excellent condition, and a complete small altarpiece by Lippo Memmi, the "Madonna and Child" with a small painted arcade across the lower one-sixth of the panel; under the arches are four saints and a praying nun, perhaps representing the order that was donor of the altarpiece.

Above: THE RAPE OF EUROPA by Titian (Tiziano Vecelli) (c. 1477-1576). Oil. The Gardner Museum's Titian Room is named for this large work, one of the finest in the collection. It portrays a Greek myth repeated in Ovid's "Metamorphoses." Zeus, in love with the Phoenician maiden, Europa, changes himself into a bull and appears as a docile animal on a shore where she is at play with other maidens. She places flowers on his head and mounts to his back. Slowly at first, so as not to frighten her, he walks into the water, then swims away to Crete, revealing himself king of the gods. *Isabella Stewart Gardner Museum.*

Adjoining the Early Italian Room on the second floor is the Raphael Room, so-named for a "Pietà" and the portrait of "Count Tommaso Inghirami," both by Raphael. The portrait is thought to have been painted in 1512, the year when Count Inghirami became Secretary to the Lateran Council and the College of Cardinals. Mrs. Gardner bought the picture from the Inghirami family in 1898. The Raphael Room also holds "The Annunciation" by Antoniazzo Romano.

The same room contains Botticelli's "The Tragedy of Lucretia" and the actively composed tempera painting on a panel, "St. George and the Dragon" (p. 12), by Crivelli, its winged dragon standing upright although impaled by part of the knight's broken lance, while St. George prepares to give the *coup de grâce* with his broadsword.

In the Titian Room, on the third floor, is "The Rape of Europa," undoubtedly one of the finest works in the collection. It is a large canvas measuring 70-by-80 inches, painted in Venice late in the artist's long life (c. 1477-1576) for Philip II of Spain. In a lively composition Zeus, in the form of a bull, strides out to sea with the plump Europa sprawled on his back, convoyed by cupids, two winging over head while a third follows astride a porpoise.

This great work came to Mrs. Gardner as a consolation in place of Thomas Gainsborough's famous "Blue Boy." She had loved the latter ever since she had first seen it in 1879 in Grosvenor House in London. In 1895 she asked Berenson to try to obtain it for her. She offered $190,000 and its owner seemed about ready to sell, but finally decided not to do so. The Titian

Above: DEATH AND ASSUMPTION OF THE VIRGIN by Fra Angelico (1387-1455). *Isabella Stewart Gardner Museum.*

Below: BINDO ALTOVITI by Benvenuto Cellini (1500-1571). Bronze. Bust of banker and art patron is one of Cellini's few authentic works. *Isabella Stewart Gardner Museum.*

had become available shortly before this for about $100,000, but Berenson, thinking Mrs. Gardner was about to spend $190,000, felt she couldn't afford the Titian too and recommended it to another collector. After the "Blue Boy" negotiations fell through, Berenson realized that Mrs. Gardner would not want to miss the Titian also, and asked her to cable him her acceptance so that it would precede the other collector's written one. She did, but apparently was never completely consoled, although today almost everyone would agree that the Titian is much the finer picture.

The other chief work in this room is Benvenuto Cellini's portrait bust of Bindo Altoviti, cast in bronze about 1550, later than his famed Perseus. The bust is mentioned in Cellini's famous *Autobiography* where the sculptor quotes Michelangelo's praise for the portrait, although, according to Cellini, he received no payment for his labors and had only the satisfaction of income from some money invested with the banker Altoviti.

On the same floor, in the Long Gallery, is Botticelli's "Madonna and Child with the Eucharist," painted around 1472, in which the Eucharist is symbolized by ears of wheat and clusters of grapes under the Madonna's hand.

While older and very famous paintings dominate in the collection, there are artists of the 19th and 20th centuries whose works are included, in addition to Whistler and Sargent.

Pictures in the ground-floor galleries and the Short Gallery on the second floor are by Mrs. Gardner's contemporaries, many of whom were personal friends or acquaintances of hers. Edouard Manet's portrait of his wife and his painting of a man in a café, landscapes by Gustave Courbet and Jean Baptiste Camille Corot, "She Goat" by Rosa Bonheur, many paintings and prints by Anders Zorn, "The Flax Spinner" by Jean François Millet, a charcoal portrait by William Morris Hunt and etchings by Charles Meryon add variety. There are no less than six works by Edgar Degas, two pencil and watercolor sketches for costumes by Leon Bakst and a painting by Henri Matisse, "Terrace, St. Tropez."

Examples of tapestries, textiles, furniture, ceramics, rare books and manuscripts, as well as memorabilia are numerous, excellent and often fascinating. The museum continues its dedication to the education and pleasure of the public even to such amenities as daily concerts and flowers from its own greenhouse.

Isabella Stewart Gardner Museum: Boston, Mass. Open Tuesday, Thursday and Saturday, 10 a.m. to 4 p.m.; Sunday, 2 p.m. to 5 p.m. Closed Monday, Wednesday and Friday (except for guided tours), all national holidays, month of August.

Above: THE CONCERT by Jan Vermeer (1632-1675). Oil. Balance, exquisite simplicity and a genius for capturing color in light are inherent in Vermeer's masterful works. Not a prolific painter, the Dutch craftsman was forgotten until, in 1866, French critic Théophile Thoré Bürger rediscovered him and became the first Vermeer historian. It was from his collection, sold at a Paris auction in 1892, that Mrs. Gardner acquired the painting early in her collecting career. *Isabella Stewart Gardner Museum.*

NEW BRITAIN MUSEUM OF AMERICAN ART

In another American cultural success story, industrial New Britain, Connecticut, is the fortunate beneficiary of a notable series of gifts which have been essential in creating the New Britain Museum of American Art. Begun in 1903 with the John Butler Talcott Fund, providing for the "purchase of modern paintings in oil by American artists," it gained the advantage of an early start in the race to collect American art and faced the hazards, implicit in the word "modern," of making the right selections in advance of the judgment of time.

During the first three decades only 23 paintings were purchased and the pictures were hung in the New Britain Institute Library in a small second-floor room. Then, in 1935, the collection was granted a great new future with the establishment of the Grace Judd Landers Fund and began its existence as an independently housed institution in 1937 after the gift to the New Britain Institute of Mrs. Landers' home at 56 Lexington Street. Following remodeling to meet the needs of the museum, the house was opened to the public in 1938. Guided by its first director, Sanford B. D. Low, the New Britain Museum began a program of expansion and consolidation of the collections.

Among the first 23 paintings acquired through the Talcott Fund were canvases by such contemporaries as Charles Hawthorne, Frederick Waugh, Willard C. Metcalf, Guy Wiggins, Frederick C. Frieseke, Childe Hassam and Arthur B. Davies. With the new resources, the director was able to reach back to include earlier American artists, among them Gilbert Stuart, Thomas Sully, John Trumbull, Samuel F. B. Morse, John Smibert and Mather Brown, all represented by portraits, Raphaelle Peale by a still life, and Benjamin West by a classical subject, "Thetis Bringing Armour to Achilles."

At the same time, Mr. Low greatly enlarged 20th-century holdings, collecting works by nearly every prominent American painter. Between 1937 and 1953 more than 300 new pictures entered the collection, and their quality and range give high testimony to Sanford Low's judgment and skill in acquisition.

During this expansive period other gifts came to the museum. The Harriet Russell Stanley Memorial was established by industrialist Alix W. Stanley in 1942 in memory of his wife. His numerous gifts to the museum were capped by his providing funds in 1950 for the first major addition to the original building. The Alix Stanley Gallery is the museum's largest exhibition space, housing the temporary exhibitions that change every month from October through June and also lec-

tures and social functions that contribute to the cultural life of the community.

In 1964 a second wing was added, given in memory of Philip B. Stanley by his wife, in which, at last, Thomas Hart Benton's huge "Arts of Life in America" murals could be installed permanently where they can be viewed together with others of his works. The four murals, eight feet high and totaling 55 feet in length, had been purchased by Alix Stanley in 1953 from The Whitney Museum of American Art for which they were painted in 1932. With the complete collection of Benton's 68 lithographs, a tempera portrait of Denys Wortman, his black and white oil sketches for the murals and all of Benton's illustrated books, the museum boasts a unique concentration of the work of this important American artist.

Another special holding of about 50 paintings and drawings is The Sanford Low Memorial Collection of

Below: THE BUTTERFLY GIRL by Winslow Homer (1836-1910). Oil. Although he often created visual representations of ordinary people and innocent pastimes, Homer's candor and freshness set him apart. *New Britain Museum of American Art.*

E. Irving Blomstrann

Above: MAIN STREET, GLOUCESTER by John Sloan (1871-1951). Oil. The paintings of "The Eight" or the Ashcan School, of which Sloan is representative, were once considered controversial and insignificant because they portrayed the everyday world, even its more unwholesome and seamy aspects, with uncompromising realism. The highly individualistic group is now acclaimed as founder of the first American school of painting in the 20th century. *New Britain Museum of American Art.*

American Illustration, originated by the museum's first director a few years before his death in 1964. His successor, Charles B. Ferguson, and a committee of illustrators and museum personnel continue to add to this collection of works by America's best magazine illustrators of the 20th century.

Although it is tempting to list the names of all the important American artists whose works can be seen in the New Britain Museum, there are too many to allow justice to all. Acquisition policy includes filling in gaps in any period, and so the collection grows rapidly in depth as well as in contemporary fields. The museum now holds more than 800 oil paintings, watercolors, drawings, prints and sculptures, broadly extending the original restriction to "modern paintings in oil by American artists."

American painting of the 19th century is very well represented by more than two dozen primarily scenic pictures by members of the Hudson River School. Six are by George Inness alone, two by Albert Bierstadt, four by Alexander H. Wyant, and there are single works by Thomas Cole, Frederick E. Church, John Quidor and others. In addition to a number of 19th-century genre paintings, there are interesting pictures by the important *tromp l'oeil* realists William M. Harnett, John F. Peto and John Haberle.

New Britain owns a particularly notable representation of "The Eight," also called the Ashcan School, who were once controversial but have long been acclaimed as founders of the first American school of painting in the 20th century. Robert Henri, John Sloan and the others of this group rebelled against the domination of the National Academy with a sensational New York exhibition in 1908 that traveled to Philadelphia, Chicago, Detroit and other cities.

It is difficult to believe that paintings by "The Eight" were once considered ugly and insignificant by "official" opinion. Each of these artists had a notably individual style, but in popular estimation they had in common an insistence upon painting from the ordinary world about them in candor — including the uncouth and awkward facets of the scene. In fact

Above: REV. JONATHAN MAYHEW WAINWRIGHT by John Trumbull. (1756-1843). Oil. Trumbull, the aristocratic and some-what pretentious son of a Connecticut governor, gained his first interest in art from the needlepoint work of his sisters. Painting was not considered a suitable occupation for men, but the young man could not stifle his desire both to copy and to create. He became a visual recorder of the people and events of the Revolutionary period. *New Britain Museum of American Art.*

Lawson was an idyllic landscape painter, Prendergast depicted pleasant scenes in his own impressionist manner, while Davies delighted in visions of classical figures in pastoral settings. It was the work of the others that was "ugly and brutal."

Sloan (1871-1951), like three others in the group, began his career as a newspaper artist in Philadelphia. His "Main Street, Gloucester," one of his two works in the museum, is representative of the many urban scenes he and others of the group painted. All of "The Eight" are in the collection. In addition to Sloan, there are five paintings by Henri, four each by George Luks and William Glackens, three apiece by Everett Shinn and Davies, two by Ernest Lawson and four by Maurice Prendergast. A number of graphics by these artists also are in the museum.

American "greats" such as Eastman Johnson, Thomas Eakins, Winslow Homer, Albert P. Ryder and James A. McNeill Whistler have not been neglected, while artists of the 20th century include George Bellows, Guy Pene du Bois, Marsden Hartley, Mary Cassatt, John Singer Sargent, Walt Kuhn and Grant Wood. Recent and contemporary artists whose work is shown include Dong Kingman, John Heliker, and the realists Aaron Bohrod, John Koch and the popular Andrew Wyeth, represented with five paintings.

Although, as is characteristic of American art in general, there is a lag in accepting avant-garde works, the New Britain Museum now is adding abstract expressionist paintings and graphics and may be expected to continue its original intention of acquiring modern American art.

New Britain Museum of American Art: New Britain, Conn. Open Tues. through Sun., 1 p.m. to 5 p.m. Closed Mon. and holidays.

Above: ONE MORE STEP, MR. HANDS by N. C. Wyeth (1882-1945). Oil. This dramatic scene is characteristic of the brilliant illustrator's drawings for Robert Lewis Stevenson's *Treasure Island. New Britain Museum of American Art.*

E. Irving Blomstrann

Above: PORTRAIT OF A YOUNG GIRL by William Glackens (1867-1933). Oil. The introspection and hesitancy of adolescence is delicately portrayed by Glackens, a representative of "The Eight." *New Britain Museum of American Art.*

ST. JOHNSBURY ATHENAEUM

St. Johnsbury, Vermont, lies in a countryside that often astonishes with the beauty of its foliage in the fall of the year and the easy association of its modern architecture with the buildings erected by the earliest townsmen, where being old is not fault as long as usefulness continues. It may be no surprise then to find in this small, lively town, the oldest art gallery in the United States that still stands in its original condition.

When, in 1871, Governor Horace Fairbanks gave to his fellow citizens the St. Johnsbury Athenaeum, comprised of a library and assembly hall, he already had gathered the core of an art collection that soon would need its own building. Two years later he added a small art gallery to the Athenaeum, its only known predecessors having been the Trumbull Gallery at Yale University, now gone, and the Wadsworth Atheneum at Hartford, of which an altered portion yet stands.

Visitors to the St. Johnsbury Athenaeum Art Gallery are impressed at once by its chief masterpiece, the grand ten-by-fifteen-foot canvas, "Domes of the Yosemite," painted by Albert Bierstadt in 1867. It fills an end wall of the gallery, while nearby on a marble pedestal stands the bust of Horace Fairbanks in white marble, perhaps from a Vermont quarry, carved by John Quincy Adams Ward. Other paintings on easels and sculpture on pedestals contribute to the period effect under the central arched skylight.

Albert Bierstadt (1830-1902), who was born in Dusseldorf, Germany, and grew up in New Bedford, Massachusetts, began to paint in oils at 21. Shortly thereafter he returned to spend four years in Europe, where his style developed, partially under the influence of the German romantics, and where his taste for mountain scenery was cultivated by trips in the Alps and Apennines. Back in America in 1857, he journeyed to the White Mountains with sketchbook and camera. A year later, he made, with a government expedition, his first trip to the Rockies. Bierstadt soon became famous and wealthy with his large canvases of the Western mountains. Never a copyist of nature, he exploited the picturesque aspects of scenery through such techniques as steepened declivities and dramatic light effects.

When Bierstadt's great picture entered the art gallery the triumph of the then small village was cause for dismay in New York and elsewhere. *The San*

Below: THE EMIGRANT TRAIN, COLORADO by Samuel Coleman (1832-1920). Coleman was a close friend of the Hudson River School painters and studied under Asher B. Durand. His most noted works are his Western scenes. *St. Johnsbury Athenaeum.*

Above: DOMES OF THE YOSEMITE by Albert Bierstadt (1830-1902). Oil. Visitors to the St. Johnsbury Athenaeum are impressed at once by its chief masterpiece. The huge canvas fills an end wall of the gallery facing the entrance. Bierstadt became famous and wealthy with his large pictures of the Western mountains. Never a copyist, he exploited the more picturesque aspects of scenery through such techniques as steepened declivities, perspective and the dramatic use of light. *St. Johnsbury Athenaeum.*

Francisco Call complained that the painting "is now doomed to the seclusion of a Vermont town where it will astonish the natives," but clearly they were more pleased than amazed.

Nearly 90 other paintings were added to complete the collection, including 17 copies of European masterworks. Although many galleries now have banished copies from their walls, the Athenaeum Art Gallery remains true to its heritage in showing these copies, acquired by its founder, of paintings by Rembrandt van Rijn, Raphael, Veronese and others, since the practice of commissioning copies was not unusual when the collection was formed.

At the same time, the American paintings of the Hudson River School, fashionable when acquired by Fairbanks and later neglected, have returned to favor and are recognized as an important part of the nation's cultural inheritance. The canvases by Bierstadt, Jasper Cropsey, Sandford Gifford, Asher Brown Durand, William Hart and his brother James McDougal Hart, Samuel Coleman and T. Worthington Whittredge, ensure that this collection will grow in value with the years.

An early Vermont painter of increasing reputation is Thomas Waterman Wood, born in Montpelier in 1823, who studied in Boston and Paris before settling in New York City. Elected to the National Academy in 1871, he is represented in the collection by two paintings.

The St. Johnsbury Athenaeum, designed by Colonel John Davis Hatch of New York, was renovated in 1948. The solid black walnut floors with walnut bookcases and wainscoting, the wood walls painted Tuscan red on which the pictures hang in deep gold frames, the stenciled gold trim in a Greek motif on the archways of the alcoves, and the pierced wood frieze providing ventilating outlets around the top of the gallery, make the room itself memorable.

A program for restoration of the pictures was begun in 1958 and this continues in order to maintain the gallery and the collection in the original condition that is its special charm.

St. Johnsbury Athenaeum: St. Johnsbury, Vt. Open Mon., Wed. and Fri., 10 a.m. to 9 p.m.; Tues., Thurs. and Sat., 10 a.m. to 5 p.m.

STERLING AND FRANCINE CLARK ART INSTITUTE

At the edge of a charming New England college town, set against the rolling, wooded background of the Berkshires, is the Sterling and Francine Clark Art Institute. There can be few visitors here who are not surprised and a little overwhelmed by the sparkling, low-profile, white marble building, its attractive surroundings and the collection of art inside — one of the most remarkable and highly acclaimed among the nation's smaller museums.

How can a museum, which first opened its collection to the public in 1955, achieve stature in such a short time? By what miracle does a collection located in farming country in the northwest corner of Massachusetts boast 30 canvases by Renoir alone, some of the finest Italian paintings, a collection of prints and drawings of exceptional quality, and superb examples of old silver and porcelains?

The miracle is the not unusual blend of a collector's passion to have the best and the philanthropist's desire to share his pleasure and wealth with the public. Robert Sterling Clark (1877-1956) and his wife Francine spent a lifetime building their collection. It began about 1912 with purchases of paintings while Mr. Clark was attached to the American Embassy in Paris. His taste did not run to contemporary art but rather to much earlier works and, by 1914, he had acquired what continues to be one of the chief treasures of the collection, "Virgin and Child with Four Angels" by Piero della Francesca, (c. 1416-1492), painted about 1465 on a relatively large wood panel, 42 by 30⅞ inches.

This stately group has the clarity of spatial organization for which the artist is famed. The four young angels stand in varied poses surrounding the enthroned Virgin, their wings barely indicated, yet sufficiently to establish them as celestial beings, while their vigorous bodies and individually studied features speak volumes about the painter's youthful models. The sturdy Virgin and Child, made to appear much larger than the angels, in the tradition of hierarchic proportion, also have a homely immediacy of gesture and expression that seems to bring the viewer into the scene, although with an appropriately low eye-level, as if kneeling.

Piero was considered a true master of painting in his own day, but was ignored for centuries, and has regained rightful recognition only in the past century. The reason why he was unappreciated for so long lies partly in what Bernard Berenson, who understood Piero's art better than most, once wrote: "At times you feel him to be clogged by science." Only relatively recently has it been seen that the perspective and mathematics in his paintings, obvious in his "Virgin and Child with Four Angels," have both a lyrical and personal value. Piero's art is strongly individual in its poetry, contemplative spirit and in the intellectual force conveyed by its abstract treatment of space and form.

With the acquisition of the "Pietà" by Perugino and a "Portrait of Gilles Joye" by Hans Memling, the group of early paintings began to grow until it now includes works by such masters as Domenico (for whom Piero was once an assistant) and Ridolfo Ghirlandaio, Benozzo Gozzoli, Luca Signorelli, Andrea da Solario (p. 12), Jan Mostaert, Jan Provost and Jan Gossaert, called Mabuse.

A special glory of the Clark Art Institute is the Ugolino seven-part altarpiece (p. 14), acquired in 1962, showing the Madonna and Child with Saints Francis, Andrew, Paul, Peter, Stephen and Louis of Toulouse. It was painted in 1321 when St. Louis of Toulouse was canonized, and yet prior to Ugolino da Siena's only fully authenticated work, the altarpiece for Santa Croce in Florence with which it has affinity, and which probably was commissioned soon after the church

Below: AT THE CONCERT by Pierre Auguste Renoir (1841-1919). Oil. Renoir took great joy in humanity and in painting the women whose soft, feminine likenesses he infused with great richness and warm color. Courtesy of the *Sterling and Francine Clark Art Institute,* Williamstown, Massachusetts.

was opened. In the words of John Pope-Hennessy, Director of the Victoria and Albert Museum: "From the standpoint of quality, size, preservation and completeness, this hitherto unrecorded altarpiece is one of the most important Sienese paintings of its time."

Siena, though a provincial town, was a great center of Italian painting from the 13th through the 15th centuries, for a time rivaling its larger neighbor, Florence. The primary characteristics of the Sienese School are subtle charm and a harmonious, decorative beauty of line and opulent color.

Dutch and Flemish paintings of the 17th century owned by the institute include works by Rembrandt van Rijn, David Teniers the Younger, Sir Anthony van Dyck, Jacob S. van Ruysdael and Peter Paul Rubens, while among French paintings of the 17th and 18th centuries two in particular are exceptional. One is the serene landscape by Claude Lorrain, a vista of a castle and trees with distant hills, and in the foreground a herdsman accompanied by playful goats and his dog driving cattle through a river. The other is the "Portrait of a Man," called "The Warrior" (p. 13), by Jean Honoré Fragonard, a spirited, swiftly executed

Below: ASENSIO JULIA by Francisco de Goya (1746-1828). Oil. The solemn eyes and stern mouth in this striking work which was painted in 1814 convey something of the legendary Spanish intensity of feeling. Courtesy of the *Sterling and Francine Clark Art Institute*, Williamstown, Massachusetts.

characterization that is one of a set of 14 "Portraits of Fantasy." It is a masterpiece of free brushwork that nonetheless blocks and models solid forms in light and shade.

Of the institute's several paintings by Francisco de Goya, one especially is likely to impress the visitor. the striking portrait, "Asensio Julia," painted in 1814. The solemn eyes and stern mouth convey something of legendary Spanish intensity of feeling.

Among the English paintings are a tiny, 6¾-by-10-inch oil, "Distant View of Salisbury Cathedral," by John Constable, inscribed on the back, "Painted on the spot, November 19th, 1821, John Constable," and his much larger landscape, "Malvern Hall." There are portraits by Thomas Gainsborough and Sir Thomas Lawrence, and impressive seascapes by Wilson Steer and J. M. W. Turner. The latter's "Rockets and Blue Lights," a dramatic incident of ships and sea, has been in a number of important exhibitions since its first showing at the Royal Academy, London, in 1840.

But it is the collection of about 150 French impressionist paintings of the 19th century that has brought the institute its greatest acclaim. Among them are Renoir's well-known and widely exhibited "Bather Arranging Her Hair," "The Ingenue" and "At the Concert." Taken altogether they offer an extremely rich and rewarding review of the work of a painter who played an independent role in the impressionist movement.

In many ways the collection demonstrates that Robert Sterling Clark was no ordinary collector, but very perceptive, willing to lead and to back his judgment with substantial purchases. Not only in his early acquisitions of Italian and Flemish art, but throughout his life he collected more than the approved and much sought-after paintings. The numerous Renoirs, the first bought in 1916, could not miss being important, but concurrently Clark acquired paintings in the realist tradition, examples of academic genre painting, and works of the Barbizon School. He purchased his first still life by Fantin-Latour in 1912, adding another in 1941, and acquired the still life, "Flowers in Blue Bowl," by Adolphe Joseph Monticelli, in 1927.

Late in his collecting, in the early 1940's, Mr. Clark became interested in the often neglected French artists of the 19th century, including the Barbizon painters. He acquired pictures by Adolphe William Bouguereau at a time when that artist's quite estimable achievement was thoroughly discredited in 20th-century eyes. Two paintings by Jean Léon Gérôme also entered the collection in this period, joining one acquired in 1930, their Near Eastern subjects important as forerunners of French fascination with the Arabic world. In the same vein is Eugène Fromentin's "Arabs Watering Horses."

Meanwhile, works by highly regarded French artists were added to the Clark collection, among them seascapes by Gustave Courbet; landscapes and figure paintings by Jean Baptiste Camille Corot, including early examples much-prized for solidity of form; landscapes by Charles-François Daubigny; and pictures from the atelier of Honoré Daumier. A fine group of 15 works by Edgar Degas shows his art in full range, with portraits, dancers and race horses painted on canvas as well as cast in bronze, among which is "The Ballet Dancer, Dressed," a pert bronze figure clothed in a fabric ballet costume.

Edouard Manet, Théodore Géricault, Jean Louis Forain, Claude Monet, Camille Pissarro, Henri de Toulouse-Lautrec and Berthe Morisot are well represented in the painting collection and also by drawings and prints.

Despite the dominance of French art, American painters are not ignored. More than 30 works by Winslow Homer provide a broad cross section of his art, including such canvases as "Undertow," and its preliminary sketches, and "Two Guides" and "Eastern Point, Prout's Neck."

While two paintings by Mary Cassatt are natural enough in a French context, the large number of pictures by John Singer Sargent must be recognized as another example of Mr. Clark's happy faculty of collecting the works of major artists during the period of their temporary eclipse.

The Clark Art Institute offers yet another attraction in a large collection of first-rate drawings, ranging from the 16th into the 20th century. The names of Albrecht Dürer, Fra Bartolommeo, Rembrandt, Rubens, Gainsborough and Thomas Rowlandson, François Boucher, Fragonard, Jean-Baptiste Greuze, Pierre Paul Prud'hon, Jean Antoine Watteau and Giovanni Battista Tiepolo may give an idea of the richness of the 16th-, 17th- and 18th-century representation.

Although the Clark Art Institute's collections rarely extend into the 20th century, a remarkable group of prints was acquired in 1962. It concentrates on the last third of the 19th century and includes a few fine works of the 20th century, among them a rare early impression of Picasso's "The Frugal Repast," dated 1904. A group of woodcuts by Gauguin would be enough to give distinction to the collection but it is also rich in prints by Pierre Bonnard, Édouard Vuillard, Edvard Munch and James Ensor.

Finally, Mr. Clark's interest in old silver provided the art institute with a large and important collection of fine pieces, highlighted by more than 50 examples of the work of the famed 18th-century English silversmith, Paul De Lamerie. Since 1962, the founders' collection has been augmented by acquisition of old English and early American pieces of an equally high quality.

Sterling & Francine Clark Art Institute: Williamstown, Mass. Open Tuesday through Sunday, 10 a.m. to 5 p.m. Closed, month of Feb.

Below: SKETCHES OF ANIMALS AND LANDSCAPES by Albrecht Dürer (1471-1528). Pen and black ink; blue, gray and rose wash. Impeccable craftsmanship and a passion for minute observation make Dürer's detailed and realistic drawings of plants and animals among the finest of his works. Courtesy of the *Sterling and Francine Clark Art Institute*, Williamstown, Massachusetts.

Above: VIRGIN AND CHILD WITH FOUR ANGELS by Piero della Francesca (c. 1416-1492). Wood panel. This stately group has the clarity of spatial organization for which the artist is famed. The four young angels stand in various poses around the enthroned Madonna, their wings barely indicated, yet enough to establish themselves as celestial beings. The sturdy Child and Mother have a homely immediacy of gesture and expression which seem to bring the viewer into the scene of protective adoration, giving it a personal value. Courtesy of the *Sterling and Francine Clark Art Institute*, Williamstown, Massachusetts.

33

WORCESTER ART MUSEUM

In tune with the public-spirited generosity that appeared among the leading citizens of many American cities and towns in the last decades of the 19th century, a group of civic leaders and civic-minded citizens united in 1896 to create an art museum in Worcester, Massachusetts. Acquiring both European and American art in the early years with the aim of building a major collection, subsequent physical enlargement of the Worcester Art Museum and redefinition of goals led to the ambitious program, now in effect, of providing an overview of art from ancient to modern times by means of the finest examples available from each school and period. These aims and policies have given Worcester a distinguished art museum that has grown in stature decade by decade, guided by clearly outstanding men serving as directors and trustees.

An example of "pop" art, Tom Wesselmann's "Great American Nude, No. 36," painted in 1962 and acquired in 1965, can be placed in the perspective of four and a half millennia in comparison with the "Female Torso" by an unknown Egyptian sculptor of the Fourth Dynasty (2680-2560 B.C.), which entered the collection in 1934. Both are about life size and both are under the same roof. Whether the "Great American Nude," a collage of fabrics, colored prints, enamel and polymer paint, possesses the qualities needed to survive for a thousand

Below: GREAT AMERICAN NUDE, NO. 36 by Tom Wesselmann (1931-   ). Enamel and polymer paint, velvet and rayon fabrics with colored prints on composition board. This reclining woman is one of a group of over 90 works by the "pop" artist deriving from the same theme, each different in form and media. In the background is a Matisse still life. *Worcester Art Museum.*

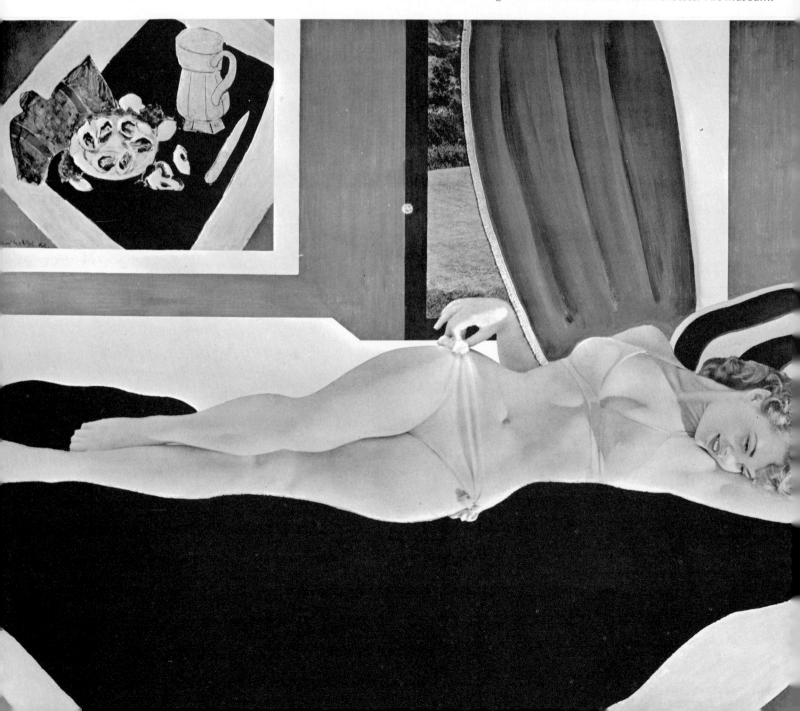

years can only be conjecture, but the Egyptian limestone figure surely is subtly and beautifully formed and is one of the finest sculptures in the collection. Between these two works stand great riches of Western and Eastern art, comprising painting, sculpture, drawings, prints and minor arts.

In 1896 Stephen Salisbury III called upon friends and associates to form a corporation for the purpose of founding an institution of art, and when the original museum building opened its doors to the public on May 10, 1898, he could not have foreseen the museum of many splendors he would inspire. But when he died in 1905 Mr. Salisbury made provision for the realization of his dream by leaving the greater part of his fortune to the museum. The income from that munificence,

augmented by later bequests and gifts, provides for maintenance and acquisitions, aided to be sure by contributions for membership by more than 5,500 persons and the money raised for the Annual Development Fund.

As with other growing museums, the need for new and renovated gallery space led to additions in 1921 and 1933. The latter, a truly major addition in the classical style of the Italian Renaissance, provided 20 new galleries arranged around a central court which house the greater portion of the museum's collection of more than 340 European paintings, 400 American paintings, and numerous examples of the other arts. There was extensive remodeling in 1940, and the latest project, in the design stage in 1966, is the addition for the museum's school and Division of Education.

Below: FEMALE TORSO. Egypt, Fourth Dynasty (2680-2560 B.C.) Subtly carved and beautifully formed, this sculpture is possibly the museum's finest. *Worcester Art Museum.*

Below: Statuette. Sumeria, Early Dynastic (3000-2500 B.C.). This archaic bearded figure with large eyes, discovered in Iraq, is the museum's most ancient work. *Worcester Art Museum.*

Looking back, Daniel Catton Rich, director since 1958, recently noted that in the first three decades of its existence the museum's acquisitions were scattered, emphasizing early Italian and contemporary American painting among other things, but without much of a plan. Then, in 1933, when the collection was rehung in the new galleries surrounding the court with the intention of presenting art through some 50 centuries, it became apparent that there were weak spots and gaps in the collected works. Although by that time the proportion of museum income that could be devoted to acquisitions had shrunk in relation to mounting costs of maintenance and administration, the trustees and directors have since labored to round out and balance the collections with the best works of art available.

The most ancient piece in the museum is a limestone statuette carved in Sumeria between 3,000 and 2,500 B.C., of an archaic bearded figure, hands folded across his middle, with large eyes, altogether an impressive figure of authority. It was acquired for Worcester in 1937, the year it was discovered beneath the floor of a temple at Khafaje, northeast of Baghdad, during excavations by an archeological expedition from the University of Pennsylvania.

The first-floor galleries of ancient and classical art also contain an Assyrian relief from the palace of Ashurnasir-pal at Calah and two early Grecian grave sculptures in marble. In the central court are seven Roman floor mosaics from Antioch-on-the-Orontes, discovered during the 1930's by an expedition sponsored by several museums, one of which was the Worcester Museum. The galleries that house art from Persia, India, China and Japan contain some of the museum's recent acquisitions, among them a wooden "Eleven-headed Kwannon" from 9th- or 10th-century Japan, standing nearly six feet high; an imposing seated "Brahma" in granite from India of the Chola Dynasty (907-1053 A.D.); and, also from India, a 12th-century Bengalese relief sculpture of Vishnu carved in schist.

For those interested in historic architecture, the Worcester Art Museum offers an unusual attraction, the 12th-century French Romanesque Chapter House,

Below: THE LAST SUPPER WITH THE AGONY IN THE GARDEN. Italy (late 13th century). Fresco transferred to canvas. The museum collection contains a number of important paintings dated before 1600, including this large, stylized fresco from the Church of Santa Maria inter Angelos near Spoleto, with detail of the Agony in Gethsemane. *Worcester Art Museum.*

Above: THE REST ON THE FLIGHT INTO EGYPT by Quentin Massys (c. 1465-1530). Oil. A prime example of 16th-century Flemish art, this painting was part of a large altarpiece, "Seven Sorrows of the Virgin," which Massys was commissioned to paint for a convent in Portugal. He depicted the rest, a popular subject, not idyllically, but as a brief respite from hardship. *Worcester Art Museum.*

originally from Le Bas-Nueil, near Poitiers, with its medieval vaulting, acclaimed "as fine and complete an example as can be seen in America."

Nearby are early European paintings of which a number of important pieces are dated before 1600. Two are large 13th-century frescos from the Church of Santa Maria inter Angelos near Spoleto, transferred to canvas: "The Last Supper" with a detail of the Agony in the Garden and "The Crucifixion." "The Madonna with Child in the Rose Garden," with its heavenly accompaniment of angels amid flowers, is a panel painting attributed to Stefano da Verona. "The Discovery of Honey" by Piero di Cosimo and "Portrait of a Man" by Giovanni Battista Moroni are others among the comparatively strong representation of Italian painting. From the 17th century the outstanding Italian picture is the dramatically lighted "The Calling of Matthew"

by Bernardo Strozzi, a large oil on canvas.

"The Rest on the Flight into Egypt" by Quentin Massys (c. 1465-1530) is the prime example of 16th-century Flemish art, a beautiful work painted on a panel that was one of seven panels of a large altarpiece of the "Seven Sorrows of the Virgin," which Massys was commissioned to paint about 1512 for a convent in Portugal. The theme of the Holy Family resting during their flight to Egypt, which first appeared in Flemish painting about 1500 and soon became a popular subject, is usually represented as idyllic, but Massys depicted it as a brief respite from hardships. This work also differs from other pictures of this subject in the prominence given Joseph and his highly personalized features. The most famous artist of his generation in Flanders, Massys was one of the first to emphasize the formal elements of design of the Italian Renaissance.

Although Dutch paintings were first acquired in the 1920's, they continued to be collected over the years. Among the later acquisitions are "The St. Bavo Church in Haarlem" by Pieter Saenredam and "St. Bartholomew" by Rembrandt van Rijn. Spanish painting, beginning with an altar frontal from Catalonia, is represented by only a few but excellent examples, among them El Greco's "The Repentant Magdalene" and "Bishop Miguel Fernandez" by Francisco de Goya.

Although French painting has not been stressed in the museum's collecting, there are 18th-century works of interest. Jean Honoré Fragonard's "The Return of the Drove" was among the notable paintings bequeathed in 1940 by Theodore T. and Mary G. Ellis, whose collection of paintings, furniture and ceramics proved to be one of the most important additions to museum holdings. "Le Geste Napolitain," dated 1757, by Jean-Baptiste Greuze, was acquired recently, as was "Sunset" by Georges Rouault. The late 19th-century French painters are represented mainly by two works of Claude Monet; "The Sulking Woman," a characteristic Tahitian canvas by Paul Gauguin; and by less important pieces by Paul Cézanne and Pierre Auguste Renoir.

An interest in English art, allied to American painting as it was, brought some important English work of the 18th and 19th centuries into the museum. Portraits by William Hogarth, Sir Thomas Lawrence and the less well-known Francis Cotes, are matched by "A Grand Landscape" by Thomas Gainsborough, an oil on canvas almost five feet square.

American painting long has held claim to priority at Worcester and therefore 17th-, 18th- and 19th-century works of quality and interest are prominent in its collection. About 1674 an unknown Boston artist made the portrait of Mrs. Elizabeth Freake and the doll-like Baby Mary, as well as the portrait of Mr. John Freake. Both of these portraits have a clear-cut outline and costume detail which are reminiscent of 16th- and early 17th-century English works. Another early family is represented by Captain Thomas Smith's "Self-Portrait," in a somewhat naive style, and his portrait of his daughter, a long-term loan from the American Antiquarian Society. At the turn of the century, Stephen Salisbury III gave a number of 18th- and early 19th-century portraits of his family, including Christian Gullager's painting of Mrs. Nicholas Salisbury. Earlier, in 1899, he had presented the lively unfinished oil of Mrs. Perez Morton by Gilbert Stuart. A Worcester County native, Ralph Earl, who studied painting in England, is properly included in the collection with four pictures.

In the early years of the century the American holdings grew rapidly, the roster of painters studded with such names as John Singleton Copley, Joseph Badger, George Inness, Thomas Eakins, Albert P. Ryder, James A. McNeill Whistler, Maurice Prendergast and John Singer Sargent. There are 20 works by Winslow Homer alone.

Perhaps because the Worcester Art Museum had started out to build a collection of world art, its first directors overlooked what was closest to home, and so

Below: FISHING BOATS, KEYWEST by Winslow Homer (1836-1910). Watercolor. The sea provided a constant inspiration for Homer and he painted it many times, in Florida, and on the Maine coast, both when it was at its most dramatic, setting the scene for man's elemental conflict with nature, and when it was at rest, as in this tranquil harbor. *Worcester Art Museum.*

it was not until the 1940's that landscapes by the members of the Hudson River School were actively sought out for the museum. All told, there are approximately 170 American paintings in the museum which date prior to the 20th century. Contemporary American paintings, together with modern European works, are shown in a separate gallery.

Although dominated by the painting collection, other fields of art are not neglected. The museum holds examples of European and American sculpture from medieval times to modern, as well as a small but significant collection of old master drawings. The decorative arts include such treasures as "The Last Judgment," a Flemish tapestry of about 1500 and a silver service made by Paul Revere. Pre-Columbian art has long been collected, and a new gallery of Japanese art is planned.

The Worcester Art Museum has been fortunate in its directors. Through the earliest years John Greene Heywood held the post of manager, followed by Frederick S. Pratt as acting manager, before appointment in 1908 of the first director, Philip J. Gentner. The eminent Francis Henry Taylor served from 1930 to 1940, when he became director of the Metropolitan Museum of New York. He was followed by Charles H. Sawyer and George L. Stout. Mr. Taylor returned as director in 1955 continuing until his death in 1957. In 1958 Daniel Catton Rich became director, after a distinguished career in the same position at The Art Institute of Chicago.

Below: WILLIAM CARPENTER by Ralph Earl (1751-1801). Oil. A Worcester County native, Earl recorded in portraiture the gentry of the Revolutionary era. *Worcester Art Museum.*

Above: HEAD OF KWAN-YIN. China, Sung Dynasty (960-1280). Wood. The goddess of mercy was a popular subject for Chinese sculpture over many centuries, each representation of her showing sympathy and compassion, as though she were truly taking a personal interest in the abundance of prayers addressed to her image. *Worcester Art Museum.*

Worcester Art Museum: Worcester, Mass. Open Monday through Saturday, 10 a.m. to 5 p.m.; special exhibitions, Tuesday until 10 p.m., October through April. Closed July 4, Thanksgiving and Christmas.

II MIDDLE ATLANTIC

ALLENTOWN ART MUSEUM

Small art museums in America literally have been created, or have suddenly expanded and flowered, following the gift of a collection from an individual donor, a corporation or a foundation. The Allentown Art Museum is one of those created by a gift, and stands alone among all the regional museums in having received in 1960 from the Samuel H. Kress Foundation a major donation of art in the form of a memorial collection. Its purpose was to honor the Kresses who were natives of Allentown.

After asking the foundation for a single picture for use in art class studies, the city received instead 16 Italian paintings, 18 northern European paintings and three German sculptures, all of the period from 1350 to 1750, forming a "study collection" that was the impetus for the creation of a museum of art.

In a handsomely remodeled church building and adjoining structure the museum has two permanent galleries for the Kress Collection and also a large main gallery and three small galleries for use in connection with temporary exhibitions that number about 25 annually. Some of these temporary exhibitions, organized by the museum, have been major events involving the publication of important catalogues and bringing to Allentown an awareness of the quality and variety of the fine arts.

For its opening exhibition in December 1959, the museum presented "Four Centuries of Still Life," from the 16th to the 20th centuries, drawn from the collections of some of the greatest museums of the nation. To complement the Kress Memorial Collection of paintings when it was unveiled in the new galleries less than a year later, another loan exhibit was arranged, entitled "Gothic to Baroque," which filled the temporary exhibition galleries with sculpture, prints, drawings, manuscripts and books, all of the first rank. Over the years these major showings, supplemented by other exhibitions, form the vital stuff of museum life around the permanent body of works in the Kress galleries.

From time to time the museum has presented exhibitions of recent additions to another major collection that had its premiere showing in February and March of 1963 and is the administrative responsibility of the Allentown Art Museum. At the end of 1961 Mr. and Mrs. James A. Michener arrived in Allentown to offer the museum custodial and curatorial authority over the James A. Michener Foundation Collection, consisting of contemporary American painting beginning with "The Eight," and ending with the immediate present — a constantly moving terminal point, since the collection of little more than 100 paintings in 1963 grew to nearly 250 in 1966 as new works were acquired.

All of the paintings and sculptures in the Samuel H. Kress Memorial Collection were purchased since 1928, when "Portrait of Saskia" by Rembrandt van Rijn was acquired. Another outstanding work is the spirited sketch of "The Young Fisherman" by Rembrandt's contemporary, Frans Hals, painted about 1635. The figure of the boy, with a background of beach and sea, is painted with the artist's characteristic bravura of fresh touch in wide brush strokes that boldly define form and texture.

Frans Hals (c. 1580-1666) is chiefly remembered for his spirited portraits that seize the mood of a particular moment. Painting in Holland at a time when an artist's patronage came largely from private collectors whose interests were temporal and materialist rather than religious, Hals developed a point of view and a method of painting that made the most of the dramatic instant, caught in the gesture of an individual and in scenes from everyday life. His brushwork, which seems to have been quick and casual, was in fact controlled with utmost precision, for he managed to capture even the appearance of laughter without loss of spontaneity by a combination of adroit draftsmanship and accurate placement of pigment that amounts to genius. Marking its importance, Allentown's "The Young Fisherman" journeyed back to Holland in 1937 at the invitation of the Frans Hals Museum of Haarlem for a special exhibition.

Among the pictures in "Four Centuries of Still Life" was "The Larder with Figures" by Frans Snyders, a great canvas almost seven feet high and eleven feet wide, borrowed for the occasion from the Kress Collection in New York. It returned to Allentown as part of the permanent collection. The painting portrays a low table laden with game, fowl, fish and vegetables, contemplated by a man and a woman. These figures are assumed to be by another hand, identity unknown, while the rest of the picture is by Snyders, whose specialty was still life and who sometimes was hired to paint still-life details in Rubens' pictures.

The list of northern European paintings includes two portraits by Jan Gossaert, called Mabuse; the painting of an interior with three men at a table, titled "The Village Lawyer," by Adriaen van Ostade; a ro-

mantic landscape of craggy wooded hills, with a stretch of water and a rushing waterfall in the foreground, by Jacob I. van Ruisdael; and a crowded room of old and young around a dining table, painted on a small canvas by Jan Steen, master of the humorous genre, titled "Soo de Ouden Songen" after a proverb that continues "Soo Pijpen de Yongen" — "As the old sing, the young pipe." In this lively picture the oldsters are shown singing as one boy plays the bagpipes and another the flute. As part of the byplay a small girl is pictured blowing into the spout of a teapot while a little boy and even a baby hold clay pipes.

Outstanding among the German sculptures is

Below: THE YOUNG FISHERMAN by Frans Hals (c. 1580-1666). Oil. With mixtures of seriousness and robust gaiety, Puritan pessimism and sensuality in his character, Hals' work throbs with vitality and characteristic bravura, as a self-confident Dutch nationalism attains its ultimate expression. *Allentown Art Museum,* Allentown, Pennsylvania. Samuel H. Kress Collection.

Above left: ELECTOR, GEORGE OF SAXONY by Lucas Cranach the Elder (1472-1553). Oil. After his individualistic style, little influenced by Renaissance classicism, was established, Cranach and his workshop of artists produced several portraits commissioned by wealthy German princes. *Allentown Art Museum*, Allentown, Pennsylvania. Gift of Mrs. Josephine Bay Paul.

Above right: PORTRAIT OF A LADY by Jan Gossaert (called Mabuse) (c. 1472-c. 1536). Oil. Gossaert's style was mature and suave in this portrait, which, according to tradition, is that of Lady Sheffield. Her costume indicates that the work was probably done in his middle period, around 1520. *Allentown Art Museum*, Allentown, Pennsylvania. Samuel H. Kress Collection.

"Saint Sebastian," by Gregor Erhart, an artist who, along with his great German contemporary, Albrecht Durer, helped to bring the Renaissance influence across the Alps into Germany. The quiet, relaxed pose and expression and relative anatomical accuracy of "Saint Sebastian" show that Erhart had by about 1500 left the Gothic Age behind and was approaching the Renaissance. Of all the German masters of the period, Lucas Cranach the Elder seems to have been the least influenced by Renaissance classicism. After his individualistic style became established, he and his busy workshop produced several portraits of German princes — such as " Elector , George of Saxony," now in the Allentown Museum, but not part of the Kress Collection — as well as many of the nude-filled allegories popular with these Renaissance aristocrats.

Among the Italian pictures in the Kress Collection is Canaletto's bright painting of "The Piazzetta in Venice" (pp. 48-49), a scene facing the ornate arcades of the warm-toned Ducal Palace, with a corner of the Church of San Marco at the left, and part of the Cam-

panile framing the scene at the right. Figures in colorful costumes form well calculated patterns across the Piazzetta; there is a traveling marionette show set up in a central arch of the lower arcade of the Ducal Palace; and gondolas with larger vessels are at the water's edge. Beyond a strip of blue canal the Church of San Giorgio Maggiore is silhouetted against the sky.

Canaletto (1697-1768), who was born Giovanni Antonio Canale, rose to prominence by responding to the 18th-century desire to have paintings depicting the real thing rather than the imaginary landscapes of mythology and classical history. The mind of this Age of Enlightenment was positive and curious, and found great satisfaction in Canaletto's rigorously objective composition and his fine sensitivity to light and atmosphere. His sparkling views of his native Venice, bathed in light, were particularly popular in dank England, where he also worked for a time.

Some others of the Italian group are "Portrait of a Gentleman," attributed to Girolamo Romanino of the

Brescian school, thought to have been painted in the second decade of the 16th century; the tiny 15½-by-12⅝-inch canvas, "Saint Jerome Penitent," assigned to Lorenzo Lotto, delightfully detailed in its small scale depiction of the saint in a landscape with a small dog-like lion near him; and a sizable panel painting of "The Adoration of the Shepherds," the artist of which is unknown but it was once thought to be Boccaccio Boccaccino.

As for the Michener Collection, perhaps its most interesting aspect is the range it encompasses between 1900 and the present, while representing the avant-garde throughout. Of "The Eight," Michener wrote in his introduction to the 1963 catalogue of the collection: "They went on to form the Ash Can School. I grew up to think of their work as the beginning of modern art in America; and although in adult life my artistic interest took me rather far afield, to Italy and Japan, I always carried with me a folder of colored reproductions of work by Sloan, Glackens, Prendergast and my special favorite, Robert Henri."

Michener also had strong feelings for the artists of the depression years, among them Reginald Marsh, Raphael Soyer, William Gropper, Ben Shahn and Philip Evergood, and a respect for art with social significance

Below: THE OLD MODEL by Robert Henri (1865-1929). Oil. Henri cared most for portraiture and the great drama he found in his subjects' faces. *Allentown Art Museum,* Allentown, Pennsylvania. James A. Michener Foundation Collection.

Above: ST. SEBASTIAN by Gregor Erhart (died c. 1540). Wood sculpture. The quiet, relaxed pose and expression of Erhart's figures and the approach to anatomical accuracy, classify him as a Renaissance sculptor of northern Europe who has left Gothic tradition behind. *Allentown Art Museum,* Allentown, Pennsylvania. Samuel H. Kress Collection.

that is rare among American collectors. Arthur Dove, Stuart Davis, John Marin, Louis Eilshemius, Niles Spencer, Max Weber and Gyorgy Kepes are some of the strong independents whose work he acquired.

With some preliminary hesitation Michener became convinced that the American abstract expressionists had achieved preeminence in world art, and their movement is well represented by the works of such artists as Hans Hofmann, Theodorus Stamos, Jack Tworkov, Robert Richenburg and Helen Frankenthaler, among many others. Works by color painter Morris Louis, "op" art by Richard Anuszkiewicz, construction painting by George Ortman, a seascape by Elmer Bischoff, and many other strands of contemporary American art are to be found in what James Michener regards as "a highly personal collection" and not a checklist for modern art.

Hans Hofmann (1880-1966), whose vigorously painted "Cascade" (p. 50) of 1960 is in the Michener Collection, became one of the most widely known exponents of abstract expressionism, the movement that dominated the New York scene around 1950 and influenced artists throughout the world. Hofmann was a popular teacher, first in his native Germany and then in New York where he ran his own school, and if he did not produce any outstanding pupils, he did enlist the enthusiasm of the many earnest students in his classes. They were enthralled by the principles and theories that Hofmann offered them, although he did not follow these in his own work, and such precepts as the "push-pull" of form and color in abstract painting provided the semblance of a contemporary academicism.

Allentown Art Museum: Allentown, Pa. Open Monday through Saturday, 10 a.m. to 5 p.m.; Sunday, 2 p.m. to 5 p.m. Closed month of Aug., New Year's Day, July 4, Labor Day, Thanksgiving and Christmas.

Below left: THE DEAD VETERAN by Larry Rivers (1923-   ). Oil. Below right: FROM THAT DAY ON by Ben Shahn (1898-   ). Tempera on canvas on board. These two American works illustrate the range and vitality of the growing Michener Collection which consists of 20th-century art. *Allentown Art Museum*, Allentown, Pennsylvania. James A. Michener Foundation Collection.

Above: CHATHAM SQUARE by Reginald Marsh (1898-1954). Tempera. Marsh portrayed New York in the 20th century just as Hogarth had depicted London in the 18th. An ardent student of the sprawling metropolis, he said, "This is a new city, wide open to the artist. It offers itself." *Allentown Art Museum*, Allentown, Pennsylvania. James A. Michener Foundation Collection.

ASIA HOUSE GALLERY

The arts of Asia have long since ceased to be exotic and strange to Western eyes. If there has been no recent dramatic Asian influence such as was exerted on Western painting by African sculpture in the early 20th century, the West has known reflections of the Far East since the voyage of Marco Polo. "Chinoiserie" has been recurrent in the architectural design and decorative arts of the West, while the impact of Japanese prints on artists in Europe is linked, for Americans, with the name of James A. McNeill Whistler. Inspired by the prestige enjoyed by ceramics in Japan, and influenced by Japanese ways of working clay, contemporary American and English potters have brought ceramics into the fold of the fine arts.

Exhibitions of art, ancient and modern, have played a major part in public education in recent years, reaching across borders to speak in art's international language. For one example, the luxuriant and lively forms of Indian stone carving, expressive of warm human qualities universal in appeal, especially have stirred enthusiasm and interest during exhibits in America.

In one way or another, most American museums and some collectors have acquired presentable examples of Asian art, yet few have specialized, and fewer still are devoted exclusively to Asian art as is Asia House Gallery in New York City. Asia House is doubly unusual, because it has no permanent collection and because it manages to present each year some of the nation's finest exhibitions of Asian art.

Conceived and founded by John D. Rockefeller III, and incorporated in 1957 as a non-profit organization for the purpose of bringing about better mutual understanding between Asians and Americans, The Asia Society engages in a number of activities to that end. It sponsors conferences, lectures and publications including *Asia*, its quarterly j o u r n a l distributed nationally, and the annual *Archives of Asian Art*. The Asia Society has a library for members' use with a reference section that serves as a clearing-house on Asian affairs.

One of the major activities of The Asia Society in New York is Asia House Gallery, established in 1960. The gallery occupies the second floor of the elegant, slim-lined, glass-fronted Asia House building, designed by Philip Johnson and Associates and completed in early 1960.

Between October and June of each year the gallery installs three major exhibitions, borrowing from public and private collections around the world, to present the historic art of Asia and in some instances to explore

(Continued on page 51)

Above: TARA. Nepal (late 14th century). Riveted sheet copper. The basic feminine type evolved in 7th-century sculpture is seen here in a mode that is comparable to that of 16th-century Venuses by Lucas Cranach. The ornaments differ but similar shapes are worn by a Bodhisattva—which in Buddhism is one who has attained enlightenment but postpones Nirvana. They are worshipped in certain sects and are often the subjects of painting and sculpture. Loaned to *Asia House Gallery* by the Victoria and Albert Museum, London.

Middle Atlantic Museums

Left: Wooden Sculpture. Nigeria, Yourba people. Yourba figures reflect ancient Mediterranean cultural stimuli which came to Africa from the North. On loan to the *Museum of African Art* by Mr. and Mrs. E. Clark Stillman.

Below: WINTER MORNING, MONTCLAIR by George Inness, (1825-1894). Oil. The American artist, George Inness, brought an intimate and naturalistic feeling to the numerous landscapes he created, as in this New Jersey scene. *The Montclair Art Museum.* Gift of Mrs. Arthur D. Whiteside, 1961.

Overleaf: THE PIAZZETTA IN VENICE by Antonio Canaletto (1697-1768). Oil. The artist's famous "views" show a superb grasp of spatial relationships and great skill in painting the intricate details of architecture. *Allentown Art Museum,* Allentown, Pennsylvania. Samuel H. Kress Collection, 1950.

Above: Detail from the HITOPADESHA. Nepal. (1594). Paper manuscript. The worldly wisdom of these charmingly illustrated Nepali fables was translated into 60 languages. Exhibited at the *Asia House Gallery*.

Left: CASCADE by Hans Hofmann (1880-1966). Oil. Hofmann's abstract expressionist canvases are boldly decorative. *Allentown Art Museum*, Allentown, Pennsylvania. James A. Michener Foundation Collection.

(Continued from page 46)

new fields in Asian art history. Nearly all the exhibitions are originated by Asia House Gallery, and these are the occasion for an authoritative publication on the exhibit by the specialist responsible for its selection. Sometimes the exhibitions are shared with other institutions and so travel to other cities.

An example of one of the gallery's exhibitions was "The Art of Nepal," presented in 1964. It included a 14th-century copper gilt image of Bodhisattva "Avalokiteshvara" owned by the Golden Monastery in Patan, Nepal. The lateral peaks of its crown are bent inward, pointing to the central crest which carries an image of Buddha Amitabha, the spiritual father of Bodhisattva Avalokiteshvara. Prior to sending this sculpture to New York for the exhibition, the authorities of the monastery from which it came sprinkled sindur (vermilion) powder over it to ensure a good journey. Gallery officials let the powder remain on the statue during the exhibit as a touch of special meaning as well as of color.

Also in the same exhibition was a paper manuscript with illustrations of the *Hitopadesha* of the year 1594 (p. 50). This is a book of profitable instruction that communicates its worldly wisdom by means of fables. The illustrations were done with typical Nepali charm.

Below: ALAM GUMAN AND HIS CALVES. India (c. 1614). Painting on cloth, mounted on cardboard. Mughal painting reached its zenith during the early 17th century. It is a synthesis of styles, arising from the teaching of the invading Persians, yet remaining true to essentially traditional Indian ideals. Loaned to *Asia House Gallery* by the National Museum of India.

In 1966 a rare exhibition of northern Indian painting from the 15th to 19th centuries was presented by the gallery. Among its most interesting works was "Darbar of Ravat Jaswant Singh of Devgarh" (p. 67). The ravats of Devgarh, a rich and powerful, though lesser, principality in Mewar, patronized painting and were renowned for their bulk, as is evident in this work.

A partial list of other exhibitions of recent years will indicate the caliber and kind of art one is likely to find in the gallery at Asia House. Some of these exhibitions may be remembered because they have traveled to museums and galleries elsewhere, and some because their fame has spread through publications: "Masterpieces of Asian Art in American Collections," "Haniwa," "Gandhara Sculpture from Pakistan Museums," "Rajput Painting," "Tea Taste in Japanese Art," "The Evolution of the Buddha Image," "The Art of India — Stone Sculpture," "Muslim Miniature Painting," "The Art of Mughal India," "Masters of the Japanese Print," "Mingei - Folk Arts of Old Japan," "Ancient Art from Afghanistan — Treasures of the Kabul Museum," "7,000 Years of Iranian Art," "Chinese Art from the Collection of His Majesty King Gustaf Adolf VI of Sweden" and "Fantastics and Eccentricities in Chinese Painting."

Asia House Gallery: New York, N. Y. Open Monday through Friday, 10 a.m. to 5 p.m.; Saturday, 11 a.m. to 5 p.m.; Sunday, 1 p.m. to 5 p.m.

Left: AVALOKITESHVARA. India (c. 14th century). Prior to sending the image to New York, sindur (vermilion) powder was sprinkled on it to wish it a good journey, and gallery officials wisely left it there to add meaning to the work. Loaned to *Asia House Gallery* by the Golden Monastery, Nepal.

Above: TWO WOMEN UNDER AN ARCHED GATE AND A WOMAN WITH A PARROT UNDER A TORĀNA. Afghanistan. Ivory. This panel, with the women wearing beaded aprons and heavy anklets, originally decorated a piece of wooden furniture. Loaned to *Asia House Gallery* by the Kabul Museum.

53

THE DUMBARTON OAKS RESEARCH LIBRARY AND COLLECTION

Two ancient civilizations meet in one of America's important collections, art of the Byzantine Empire and pre-Columbian art, housed in a historic building in Georgetown, the oldest section of Washington, D. C. The original house was constructed in 1801, although subsequent owners have remodeled and enlarged it many times.

When Mr. and Mrs. Robert Woods Bliss acquired the house in 1920 they named it Dumbarton Oaks, recollecting that the property was called the Rock of Dumbarton at the time of the last grant from Queen Anne to Colonel Ninian Beall in 1702. The name became known internationally in 1944, not for art but because the Dumbarton Oaks Conference was held there, a preliminary to the establishment of the United Nations in San Francisco.

The Blisses changed and enlarged the house extensively, expanded the grounds and established stately

Above: Reliquary Cross, Macedonia, Saloniki (late 12th to early 18th century). Gold and cloisonné enamel. The ancient crucifix bears the Greek words, "Jesus Christ, Lord of Glory." *Dumbarton Oaks,* Washington. Robert Woods Bliss Collection.

gardens that remain a permanent attraction. Pursuing their interest in Byzantine art, they worked to create a research center, gathering works of art and many books. To house the collection two wings were built in 1940, and in that same year the research library and the collection were given to Harvard University, so "that the continuity of scholarship in the Byzantine and Medieval humanities may remain unbroken . . . ."

Dumbarton Oaks itself became the property of The Trustees for Harvard University a year later, and during the next quarter-century both collection and library were expanded. Meanwhile, Mr. Bliss, who had acquired his first example of pre-Columbian sculpture in 1912 and had been collecting it while building the Byzantine material, turned intensively to the task of assembling this second collection, an interest he pursued until his death in 1962.

Between 1947 and 1962 the pre-Columbian objects were exhibited in the National Gallery of Art and then, at the bequest of Mr. Bliss, the collection returned to Dumbarton Oaks where it is housed in a new addition constructed in 1963, designed by Philip Johnson.

Under the direction of The Trustees for Harvard University, a District of Columbia corporation, the Dumbarton Oaks Center for Byzantine Studies conducts scholarly research through its faculty and fellows. The research library now numbers nearly 70,000 volumes, and with the collection of objects, photographic files, lectures, symposia, publications and, recently, archeological field work, the center is unequaled in its area of study. There is also a small research library in connection with the pre-Columbian collection.

The Byzantine collection, "dedicated primarily to the minor arts of the early Christian and Byzantine periods," includes objects from the classical ancient world of Greece and Rome, the ancient Near East, Christian Egypt and the medieval West. Although the original Bliss collection still forms the major part of the whole, it has been increased by half again since the initial gift to Harvard.

Examples of the arts of the Byzantine Empire, which spanned the 4th to the 15th centuries, include numerous works of sculpture in stone and bronze, metalwork, some glyptics and ivories, objects of bone, steatite and wood, glass and ceramics, enamels, mosaics, and some paintings in tempera, encaustic and fresco.

In every category are objects of great aesthetic interest, which the annotated catalogue of the collection describes and places. One of the impressive sculptures is the hollow cast bronze "Statue of a Horse," dated in the late Roman period and reportedly found at San'a, the capital of Yemen, in South Arabia. The

Above: STATUE OF A HORSE. South Arabia, Yemen (probably late Roman period). Bronze. Said to have been found at San'a, the capital of Yemen, the rearing horse originally held a rider. Inscriptions on the shoulder and rump helped identify the statue as a votive (dedicatory) figure and gave evidence for its date. *Dumbarton Oaks,* Washington. Robert Woods Bliss Collection.

rearing horse, now minus a rider, is about 40 inches high and a little longer, sensitively stylized with attention to anatomical details and lively expression.

There is a large study collection of textiles, some of which are shown and catalogued. One of these is the 6th-century Egyptian wool tapestry carrying the Greek inscription "Hestia Polyolbos" ("Hestia Rich in Blessings"). The central figure personifies the hearth; the six putti, three on each side, carry medallions naming her blessings: wealth, joy, praise, abundance, virtue and progress. Attendants to the right and left present inscribed tablets, one illegible, the other reading in Greek, "Light." The blue-green background is scattered

with flowers in rose, green and buff, the same hues that distinguish the figures, throne and medallions.

In process of being studied, leading toward cataloging, are two other collections, one of more than 4,500 gold and silver coins and medallions and the other of about 7,000 seals.

Of equal interest to many visitors, the large Robert Woods Bliss Collection of Pre-Columbian Art, in its strikingly modern building, is the fruition of half a century of collecting. Except for a few pieces, the collection was all assembled by Mr. Bliss, who was more concerned about aesthetic merit than he was about archeological value. The examples of stone carving,

Above: Panel of HESTIA POLYOLBOS. Egypt (6th century). Wool tapestry. The figure of Hestia, goddess of the hearth, described as "Hestia Rich in blessings," is enthroned between two attendants and six putti (cupidlike children), holding medallions inscribed in Greek with blessings distributed by her: wealth, joy, praise, abundance, virtue and progress. The attendant at right holds a tablet inscribed in Greek with the word, "Light." *Dumbarton Oaks,* Washington. Robert Woods Bliss Collection.

pottery, fresco, jewelry and textiles come from Mexico, Guatemala, Costa Rica, Panama, Colombia and Peru.

As for the Byzantine collection, there is an excellent catalogue of the pre-Columbian arts. However, the luxuriant forms carved in relief on stone, painted in fresco and on pottery, or cast and hammered in gold, among which are some others of classic simplicity and strength, are far from being fully understood. For example, one of the most striking pieces in the collection is a later classic Mayan figurine of a woman sitting cross-legged and with a high, elaborate headdress (p. 69). The classic Mayan civilization, which lasted for six centuries, represented the highest intellectual peak attained by the American Indian. It was located in northern

Guatemala, Honduras, and Chiapas and the Yucatán Peninsula in Mexico. The Maya were literate, but most of their writing has not been deciphered and the correct correlation between the extremely advanced Maya and Christian calendars is not certain.

There is much still to be learned and many relationships are not yet established. But whether fearsome figures of gods, startling animal forms, or appealing human effigies like the ancient Olmec head of a woman broken from a statue, there is a vitality to the pre-Columbian works that makes them live today.

The Dumbarton Oaks Research Library and Collection: Washington D. C. Collections and Music Room, open Tues. through Sun., 2 to 5 p.m.; Gardens, daily, 2 to 5 p.m. Closed legal holidays, July & Aug.

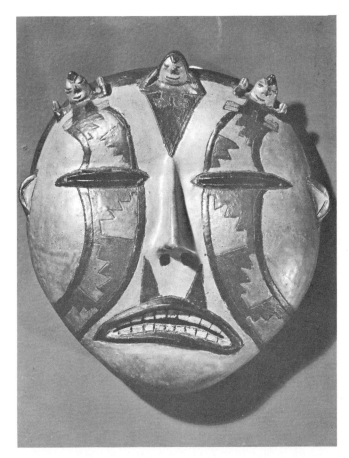

Above left: CROCODILE GOD. Colombia, Tairona Culture (1000-1500 B.C.). Cast tumbaga (an alloy of gold and copper in which the surface copper is removed to leave only the gold). The body of the god is human, while the face is probably a mask with two bird bodies over the eyes. *Dumbarton Oaks*, Washington. Robert Woods Bliss Collection.

Above right: Mask. Peru, Late Paracas Style (1st century B.C.). Pottery, polychromed with post-fired resin paint. Three human figures adorn the forehead, while two curving bands pass through the eyes and across the cheeks of this symbolic mask. *Dumbarton Oaks,* Washington. Robert Woods Bliss Collection.

Right: BUST OF A WOMAN, Mexico, Olmec Style (800-400 B.C.). Olmec, the earliest known civilization in Mesoamerica, is noted for its craftsmanship, exemplified by the realistically carved face and hair which was broken from a statuette. *Dumbarton Oaks,* Washington. Robert Woods Bliss Collection.

THE MONTCLAIR ART MUSEUM

Just as chance sometimes seems to rule the affairs of individuals it was an accident of history that set The Montclair Art Museum on its course of collecting American paintings, and subsequent circumstances encouraged the museum to continue in that enterprise.

In 1909 William T. Evans offered the Montclair Municipal Art Commission, a year after it was established, some 30 American paintings from his collection, provided that Montclair would build a suitable museum for them. Evans was an unusual but practical collector who bought pictures by his contemporaries, both because he liked their work and because he wished to support and encourage living artists. It is no matter now that many of his purchases are not at this time considered important; in fact, only five of the original 30 are highly regarded. He did, however, provide the impetus for establishment of the museum, and, although its collecting later was broadened to include 18th- and early 19th-century works, the dedication to contemporary American art continued and was vigorously renewed in 1946 when the Blanche R. Pleasant Fund was established for such purchases, with emphasis on modern developments.

Other circumstances helped, too. Perhaps because George Inness had lived and worked in Montclair, causing other artists to gravitate there, the museum received gifts of American art in goodly number, but relatively few of European art. Furthermore, its sense of direction led to a policy of actively seeking American works, although gifts of art from other cultures are accepted. For half a century New Jersey's only museum devoted entirely to art, The Montclair Art Museum now is distinguished by the importance of its still growing American collection. From 1961 to 1966 approximately 75 American paintings entered the collection by gift or purchase. While one of these, Gilbert Stuart's "Portrait of Thomas Dawson, Lord Dartrey, Viscount Cremorne," is of the 18th century, 39 are 20th century, and the rest fill gaps in the 19th-century representation.

The first response to William Evans' contingent gift came from an artist, Florence O. R. Lang, who contributed $50,000. Other gifts followed to permit construction of an appropriately designed neo-classic building, and on January 15, 1914, The Montclair Art Museum opened its doors in this suburban community 15 miles from New York.

Paintings by Childe Hassam, Theodore Robinson, T. Worthington Whittredge and Ralph A. Blakelock were among the initial 30. In the next three decades a few outstanding paintings were slowly acquired, such

Above: PORTRAIT OF CHARLES L. FUSSELL by Thomas Eakins (1844-1916). Oil. In this portrait of his friend, Eakins revealed his unusual ability to emphasize the inner life of his subjects, intensifying reality. *The Montclair Art Museum.*

as the much-reproduced "The Delaware Water Gap" by George Inness and paintings by Ernest Lawson, Arthur B. Davies and Robert Henri.

The depression years reduced purchases to just one remarkable picture, the bleak "Coast Guard Station" by Edward Hopper, in which buildings are cut into geometric abstractions by sunlight and shadows. It was painted only ten years before it was acquired in 1937.

Then in 1943 came the landmark endowment of the Florence O. R. Lang Bequest, which in a few years changed The Montclair Art Museum into one of the few centers where the nation's painting can be seen in historical depth.

It was natural for the museum to take a special interest in the work of the most prominent painter who was a Montclair resident, George Inness.

The art of George Inness (1825-1894) matured slowly. Because of an early illness he was dismissed from school. After failing as a grocer and mapmaker, he studied for a month with the French landscapist, Régis Gignoux, who lived in this country for several years. It was Inness' desire to combine the best qualities of the work of two leaders of the Hudson River School: the "lofty striving" in Thomas Cole, with Asher B.

Above: JIMMIE O'D by Robert Henri (1865-1929). Oil. Henri's portraits contain the vital quality of life, and he urged his students to strive for the same goal, both on canvas and in life. *The Montclair Art Museum*. Gift of Mrs. Estelle Armstrong.

Above: PORTRAIT OF GENERAL GEORGE WASHINGTON, by Charles Willson Peale (1741-1827). Oil. This portrait entered the museum collection after its discovery in a London attic and 178 years of neglect. *The Montclair Art Museum*.

Durand's "more intimate feeling for nature." Although Inness traveled in Europe, he agreed with the Hudson River School that the first duty of an American artist was to re-examine the American landscape. He differs from most of the Hudson River School, however, because of his more lyrical color sense. In his later years, influenced by the Barbizon School, his art — based on what he called an "impression of nature," combining the "poetry of nature" with "the objective fact" — brought him a large income as well as many honors.

Inness is represented in The Montclair Museum by ten oils, including "Winter Morning, Montclair" (p. 47), two watercolors, and 59 small sketches from his Montclair studio sketchbook. The museum also has assembled extensive reference materials about the artist, has his palette and brushes, and owns two paintings by his son, George Inness, Jr., one of which depicts "George Inness Sketching Outside His Montclair Studio," dated around 1889.

When, in 1945, the "Portrait of Caleb Whitefoord," painted by Gilbert Stuart in 1782, was acquired by the museum, this first 18th-century addition caused a fresh look at museum policies, leading to a master plan for acquisition of a historical collection of American paintings. Planning and wise purchases have built a well-balanced representation in which only the most recent of prominent American painters are not yet included.

The 18th-century group was splendidly augmented in 1960 by the purchase of Benjamin West's "Cromwell Dissolving the Long Parliament," a large five-by-seven-foot canvas of great historical interest as well as a fine example of a phase of the artist's work. This was joined a year later by a remarkable pair of portraits by Charles Willson Peale: "Portrait of General George Washington," while the subject was commander of the Revolutionary War armies, the other of General Nathanael Greene.

Charles Willson Peale (1741-1827) began his adult life as a saddlemaker and switched to portraiture only after he learned he could make more money at it. Obviously a practical man, he was annoyed by the high-flown sentiment that talent in the fine arts is an exclusive gift and cannot be acquired, which he had heard in London where he had gone to study with Benjamin West. He tried to disprove this when, later in Philadelphia, he trained several members of his family to paint quite well. A prolific man in many ways, he completed over 1,000 pictures and fathered 17 children by three successive wives before he died

Above: COAST GUARD STATION by Edward Hopper (1882-1967). Oil. This bleak painting was the one remarkable work which entered the collection of The Montclair Museum during the depression years. The buildings are cut into geometric abstractions by the interplay of sunlight and shadow, a technique which was always of primary interest to Hopper. *The Montclair Art Museum.*

at the age of 85. Among the reputable artists Charles Willson Peale trained in his family are James, his youngest brother, and sons Rembrandt and Raphaelle.

The two portraits by Charles Willson Peale in Montclair were discovered in the attic of an English family near London after 178 years of neglect. It seems that Peale had entrusted the portraits to General Joseph Reed on a trip back to England, hoping he could show them to Benjamin West. West had advised Peale to have engravings made by the London engraver, Joseph Brown. The engravings were made but the originals were not promptly returned and eventually were relegated to the attic of Reed's father-in-law's house where they were forgotten.

The earliest portrait in the museum is the "Self-Portrait" by John Smibert, done about 1728. Among other 18th-century pieces are portraits by John Singleton Copley, John Wollaston and Joseph Blackburn.

Paintings by members of the Hudson River School, some included in the original gift, and other 19-century artists were progressively increased in number until the museum can boast a very complete selection, including, in addition to the many by Inness, works by Washington Alston, Albert Bierstadt, Ralph A. Blakelock, Thomas Cole, Asher B. Durand, Eastman Johnson, John Frederick Kensett, Thomas Moran, Samuel F.B. Morse, William Sidney Mount and T. Worthington Whittredge.

Fortunate purchases in the 1920's, before the museum's ambitions extended beyond support for the contemporary artist, made it easier later to round out one important segment of American art. The acquisitions of Arthur B. Davies' painting of two little children called "Meeting in the Forest" and Robert Henri's vital sketch of a boy, "Jimmie O'D," gave the museum a head start in completing a collection of examples by all of "The Eight," those rebels against the Academy, among whom Henri was a leader, who defined a purely American strain in 20th-century painting.

Two drawings by Winslow Homer and an early portrait of a girl, the gentle "La Jeune Mariée" by Mary Cassatt, acquired between 1951 and 1961, are illustrative of the difficulties faced by a museum with limited funds in competing for works by favored artists; often it proves advantageous to be satisfied by examples from an artist's less popular periods or typical styles. Finally, in 1962, a handsome Homer watercolor added significantly to the collection.

"The Sea" by James A. McNeill Whistler, an 1865 interpretation of sea and sky that prefigures later works by the artist; an 1883 portrait by John Singer Sargent; and a composition by Marsden Hartley were important additions. "Still Life with Fruit Bowl," painted by Alfred H. Maurer about 1910, formed an early American response to the new spirit in art generated by fauvism and cubism.

An outstanding recently acquired work is Thomas Eakins' "Portrait of Charles L. Fussell." Fussell was a boyhood friend of Eakins and an artist. In this forceful, yet warm, portrait, Eakins demonstrates his ability to express the inner life of his subject. Eakins was at the center of art in America at the turn of the century, a period during which Frank Duveneck, whose "Portrait of Amy Folsom" (p. 68) in the museum shows some of the same qualities as Eakins' work, was also popular.

The 1945 gouache called "Day in Winter" by Charles Burchfield, with its lively rhythm of tree branches and fences against snow and sky, joins with "East of the Bowery, 1923" (p. 68) by Jerome Myers, "Mountain Laurel" by John Steuart Curry, "Wellfleet Pond" by Edwin Dickinson, and paintings by Stuart Davis, John Marin, William Kienbusch, Andrew Wyeth and some younger contemporaries, to bring the Montclair collection up to very recent years.

Other museum attractions are the Whitney Collection of antique English, Scottish, Irish and French silver, a permanent exhibition selected from the Rand Collection of American Indian materials, small collections of European and Oriental art and some pieces of decorative art. About 40 exhibitions are presented each year.

The Montclair Art Museum: Montclair, N. J. Open Tuesday through Saturday, 10 a.m. to 5 p.m.; Sunday, 2 p.m. to 5:30 p.m. Closed Mon.

Below: GOOSE RIVER by Andrew Wyeth (1917-   ). Watercolor. Wyeth has always been an imaginative observer of his Maine environment, sometimes painting the same subject again and again, each time with fresh perception. Homer's watercolors influenced the young painter, leading him to create dynamic and rapid impressions of light. *The Montclair Art Museum.*

Above: DELAWARE WATER GAP by George Inness (1825-1844). Oil. Inness combined the intimate feeling for nature he found in Asher B. Durand's work with the "lofty striving" of Thomas Cole, both leaders of the Hudson River School, and he felt the duty of American artists was to re-examine the landscape of their own country. *The Montclair Art Museum.* Gift of Mrs. F. G. H. Fayen.

Below: CROMWELL DISSOLVING THE LONG PARLIAMENT by Benjamin West (1738-1820). Oil. It is quite natural that West should choose this particular subject for one of his historical works since he was a great favorite in England, where he kept a studio in a magnificent London mansion, and, with noble deference, received admiring throngs. *The Montclair Art Museum.*

MUSEUM OF AFRICAN ART

Taking its place in the ranks of Washington's truly formidable museums is the unique Museum of African Art. The museum is the only one in the United States devoted exclusively to portraying the rich and ancient creative art of the Negro peoples of the world and the impact which the arts of Africa have had upon modern Western culture. In its objectives the museum reaches beyond aesthetics and art education to foster public awareness of the implications of African art in the realm of intercultural understanding.

Selected as the site for the museum was the former home of Frederick Douglass, the eminent 19th-century abolitionist orator, editor and government official. The duplex building, in the shadow of the Supreme Court on Capitol Hill, also houses the companion Frederick Douglass Institute of Negro Arts and History which sponsors the Museum of African Art.

The museum was conceived by its first director, Warren M. Robbins, who, as a cultural attaché in the United States Foreign Service stationed in Europe, had long been interested in intercultural influences and the problems of cross-cultural communication. In collecting art while in Europe during the years 1949-1960, Robbins was struck by the similarities between many works of African sculpture and of 20th-century Western art. Wider public knowledge of African sculpture and of its influence upon Western artistic developments could not but help promote respect and appreciation for Africa's cultural traditions, he felt.

Formally established in October 1964, the museum contains eight small galleries in which some 300 works of traditional African sculpture are displayed. One special gallery exhibits African art in juxtaposition with works — originals and reproductions — by Pablo Picasso, Paul Klee, Amedeo Modigliani and other artists of the cubist, fauve and German expressionist schools whose paintings and graphics manifest African derivations or parallels.

About one-third of the sculpture on display in the young museum is owned by it. The rest of the works are on long and short term loan from other museums — the University of Pennsylvania Museum, The Museum of Primitive Art, the Smithsonian, the Museum of Modern Art — as well as from private collections. While the permanent collection is being built, the policy of presenting distinguished exhibits and individual pieces on loan gives Washington residents and visitors unique opportunity to view fine works of art of African origin. One of the major loan exhibitions shown in 1966 was "Traditional African Art from the Peabody Museum of Harvard University," consisting of 150 examples of sculpture, pottery, textiles and ornaments.

Among the finest pieces in the museum is the wooden fertility figure of the Yoruba tribe (p. 47) which is on loan from a private collector. The energetic and alert Yoruba, largest of the sculpture-producing tribes in Africa and the most prolific, dwell in what is now western Nigeria and parts of eastern Dahomey. Their territory seems to have acted as a cultural focal point for much of the Egyptian, classical and early Christian-Byzantine influences that entered Negro Africa from the north. Another interesting work is the crop fertility symbol *(Chi-Wara)*, an antelope headdress made by the Bambara people of Mali. The doe antelope carries a child on her back.

The role of the Museum of African Art in strengthening the American Negro's feeling of ethnic pride in the creative accomplishments of his forebears is supplemented by exhibits in the adjacent Frederick Douglass Institute, reflecting the Negro contribution to American culture and society. These exhibits include the Frederick Douglass Memorial Room containing the original furnishings, books and documents which either belonged to Frederick Douglass or reflect his life and times. The institute also contains a children's gallery with portraits of Negroes who have made basic contributions to American life; another gallery displays works by Negro American artists of the 19th and 20th centuries.

In all of these endeavors and an active education program, the museum is fulfilling its ambitions for the cultural and social integration of the Negro and white people of America and for a deeper understanding between the peoples of Africa and the United States.

Museum of African Art: Washington, D. C. Open Monday through Thursday, 11 a.m. to 5:30 p.m.; Saturday through Sunday, 2 p.m. to 5:30 p.m. Closed Friday (except by appointment) and legal holidays.

Below: Fertility Doll. Ghana, Ashanti Tribe. Worn by a mother to assure beauty in her children. The *Museum of African Art.*

Above: Mortuary Figure. Gabon, Bakota Tribe. Copper and wood. A relief figure used to ward off evil from ancestral remains. Loaned to the *Museum of African Art* by Alan Sawyer.

Right: DOE ANTELOPE WITH CHILD. Mali, Bambara Tribe. Wood. A *Chi-Wara* crop fertility symbol with headpiece. Loaned to the *Museum of African Art* by Gaston de Havenon.

Below: FIGURES HOLDING PALM WINE CUP. Republic of the Congo, Basonge Tribe. Wood. Basonge figures are related to Bakuba carvings. *Museum of African Art*. Gift of Emil Arnold.

Cranwell

THE MUSEUM OF PRIMITIVE ART

The first museum for primitive art was established in New York City in 1957, and seldom, if ever, has a museum had such an initial impact in its chosen field.

During a century of many revolutions, including some in the arts, one of the most remarkable has been the changing point of view toward primitive peoples and their works. The indifference and complacency of the 19th century, which assumed all indigenous cultures to be inferior and prelogical, placed little value on primitive arts except as curios. Even when preserved in the great treasure houses of the natural history museums, the objects gathered as the odd, fearsome, exotic handiwork of primitive people were regarded as artifacts rather than as expressive art.

What was even worse was well-meant missionary vandalism that was enacted many times in many places. One of the most disastrous acts occurred in 1835 when missionaries destroyed en masse the carvings belonging to the people of the Gambier Islands; only seven pieces are known to have survived. The tragedy of that loss through destruction is intensified in the presence of one of the sculptures saved from the holocaust now in The Museum of Primitive Art. This half-size wooden figure probably represents a Polynesian rain god, symbolized by the rainbow, who sent rain to nourish the islands' breadfruit trees.

Now, however, the idea of the primitive has been recast to eliminate notions of crudity and immaturity, and to give recognition to the elaborate tradition, subtlety and skilled craftsmanship embodied in much of what is called primitive art.

When New York's Museum of Primitive Art first opened its doors it was the only museum of its kind. First named the Museum of Indigenous Art, to indicate its purpose of recognizing the artistic achievements of the original populations of six continents, the trustees, headed by founder Governor Nelson A. Rockefeller, later accepted the word "primitive," but not without ample explanation and interpretation. Eventually, with wider appreciation of the essential oneness of man in the role of artist and more study of primitive art, it has been suggested that "primitive" as a designation for any kind of art will no longer be useful because art now called primitive, in all its variety, will have been related to specific places and peoples.

With the example of The Museum of Primitive Art and success in its aim to select and exhibit "objects of outstanding beauty whose quality is the equal of

(Continued on page 71)

Above: PECTORAL REPRESENTING HUMAN MASK. Nigeria, Benin. Ivory, metal, stone. *The Museum of Primitive Art.*

Below: SEATED FIGURE. Mexico, Maya (410-650 A.D.). Wood and paint. Many consider Mayan art the finest of pre-Columbian America. Courtesy of *The Museum of Primitive Art.*

Middle Atlantic Museums

Left: Feather wall hangings. Peru, Coast Tiahuanaco. (c. 700 A.D.). Feather poncho. Peru, Inca. (c. 1500 A.D.). South American Indians used feathers for symbolic and decorative purposes as well as clothing. *The Museum of Primitive Art*.

Below: DARBAR OF RAVAT JASWANT SINGH OF DEV-GARH. India, Rajasthan. (18th century). A North Indian court is pictured in a style that reverts to Pre-Muslim traditions of using intense colors, brusquely painted forms and repeated patterns. Exhibited at the *Asia House Gallery*.

Left: PORTRAIT OF AMY FOLSOM by Frank Duveneck (1848-1919). Oil. Duveneck was a clever pupil of the "Munich Style." His fluent, graceful and pleasing works made him an overnight success in America. *The Montclair Art Museum.*

Below: EAST OF THE BOWERY, 1923 by Jerome Myers (1867-1940). Oil. Myers was a painter of New York's streets and slums. His pictures are tender and luminous studies avoiding the violent and sentimental. *The Montclair Art Museum.*

Right: Figure. Mexico, Jaina Style. Late Classic Maya. Clay. The figures of this period, which show great mastery in handling elaborate form, are among the most famous Mayan art objects. *Dumbarton Oaks.* Robert Woods Bliss Collection.

(Continued from page 66)

work of any time and place," the large natural history museums began to look at their collections of primitive art as aesthetic objects, to prepare exhibitions and to train museum staffs. Simultaneously, there was a marked increase in the collecting of primitive art by museums everywhere.

Of the more than 3,500 objects in The Museum of Primitive Art, including sculpture in wood, stone, bronze, precious metals, paintings, textiles, ceramics and jewelry, only a small part can be exhibited at one time. Where each piece comes from is essential to knowledge about it, yet so diverse and numerous are the origins of primitive art that it is necessary to classify the objects generally as African, Oceanic, North American, Middle American and South American. Within each major group distinctions are made by period, country, place or tribe, and purpose when known.

The complete story of the indigenous arts may never be known because so much of the material was perishable and has perished, yet persistent exploration and study is certain to make remarkable discoveries. One such discovery is the Maya wood sculpture of a seated man, probably a priest or high ranking religious functionary in a posture of adoration, only about 15 inches nigh and carved from hard, reddish-brown wood, found near the borders of Guatemala and Tabasco. It is a remarkable survival from a region where moisture quickly destroys wood, especially since stylistic considerations indicate a classic period origin. Radiocarbon dating has placed the work around 537 A.D., yet many unresolved questions remain concerning details of the carving and the significance of the piece.

Nonetheless, the compelling and enigmatic quality of expression in the face and in the gesture of the body, together with the evidence of keen observation and skill in carving, give to this figure a powerful presence that ranks it very high as a work of art.

Such qualities are to be found again and again in

Above: Figure Representing a God or Divine Ancestor. Polynesia, Marquesas Islands. Bone. Pacific cultures and the hierarchical societies of Polynesia provide disciplined and intricate objects in wood, some dating from early 19th-century explorations. Courtesy of *The Museum of Primitive Art.*

Above: SMILING HEAD. Mexico, Veracruz, Remojadas (c. 500 A.D.). Primitive art need not conjure visions of the horrible and the unknown. At times, as in this smiling face, it can be both intimate and charming, conveying a personal and amusing message. Courtesy of *The Museum of Primitive Art.*

Left: Ceremonial carvings. New Guinea, Sepik River region. *The Museum of Primitive Art.*

the fine examples displayed by the museum. One such example is the brightly colored feather wall hangings (p. 67) from Coastal Tiahuanaco, Peru, which date from about 700 A.D. Another is the group of ceremonial wood carvings (p. 70) from the Sepik River region in New Guinea. Typical of Sepik art are the exuberant swirling lines and richness of form exceeding that of works from any other part of Oceania. One motif on the elongated Sepik shield (left, background in photograph) that can be traced back many centuries to early China is the grotesque face sticking out its tongue in an evil-averting gesture.

If the rich variety of materials and styles is initially confusing in the absence of simple canons for judgment, one need only single out a few pieces for longer study, letting them communicate across the years their human qualities of vitality, beauty, humor, awe, resignation, fear and compassion.

The Museum of Primitive Art: New York, New York. Open Tuesday through Saturday, 12 p.m. to 5 p.m.; Sunday, 1 p.m. to 5 p.m.

Above: Effigy Jar. Peru, Mochica. Clay and paint. Peruvian art developed primarily in the coastal valleys, including the dominant Mochica in the north. Their figures reflect Chavinoid sculptural tradition with which they have a distant affinity. Courtesy of *The Museum of Primitive Art.*

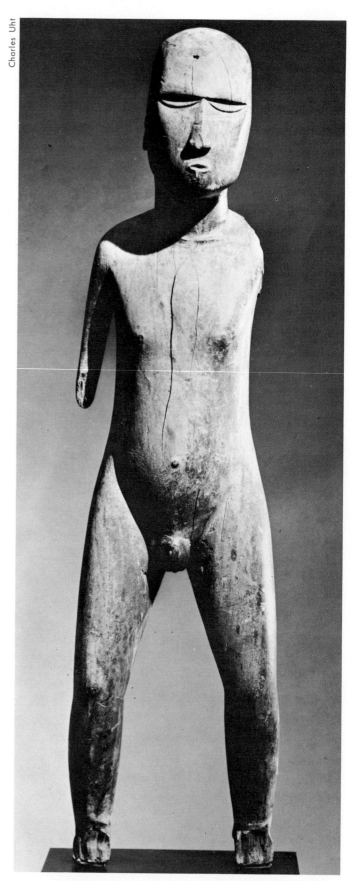

Above: FIGURE OF A GOD. Polynesia, Gambier Islands, Mangareva. Wood. This figure, which is one of a surviving few, probably represents the god Rogo or Rongo, symbolized by the rainbow, who sent rain to nourish the breadfruit trees of the islands. Courtesy of *The Museum of Primitive Art.*

Above: KNEELING FIGURE. Tennessee, Humphreys County, Duck River. Late Mississippi Culture (1300 A.D.). This kneeling male figure is one of a pair (male and female), a rare remaining statue done by the Gordon People who inhabited the region from 1000-1600 A.D. The piece was discovered on a farm in 1895 and the museum acquired it in 1957. The Gordons buried their dead in stone coffins and a pair of figures, made by the tribe's expert sculptors, were placed with the bodies. Figures from this area reflect the cultural influence of late, advanced developments in Mexico. Courtesy of *The Museum of Primitive Art*.

THE WASHINGTON GALLERY OF MODERN ART

Some museums have begun with the gift of a lifetime's collection of art, but in this day, when new museums are appearing almost every other week, some have started out with little more than brave aspirations of forming a collection. This is particularly true of museums devoted to contemporary art, since the prime material needed for their collections is so new that owners are loath to part with what has just been acquired, and much of the eligible art is still in the hands of dealers and artists. Accordingly, the founding of a truly modern museum can be a most exciting and demanding creative act for those involved. While the paintings, sculptures, drawings and prints they wish to acquire may never be easier to beg or buy, the risk of error in selection is high in the absence of time's proverbial judgment. Nevertheless, the rewards of being on the frontier of living art are very great.

One museum on the leading edge is The Washington Gallery of Modern Art, which was opened late in 1962 by a dedicated group from Washington and elsewhere with the aid of foundation grants. In the beginning the gallery concentrated on exhibitions of contemporary art, while accepting gifts for the permanent collection that by 1966 catalogued 137 examples of paintings, sculpture, drawings and prints. In accordance with the now generally accepted pattern for building museum holdings, all gifts of art are outright, and the gallery's accession committee has the privilege of acting upon the acceptance of the works of art to improve or redirect its growing collection.

No particular bias can be detected in the Gallery of Modern Art's orientation other than to be open-minded and to favor Americans two to one over foreign artists. Among the old masters of contemporary art, Josef Albers is represented by nearly two dozen prints, Juan Gris by two lithographs and Marcel Duchamp, the major-domo of modern art, by one of his 300 "portable museums," the 1938 "Valise."

At the other end of the time scale it is apparent that from the start the Gallery of Modern Art has been on the breaking wave of contemporary expression, since three out of four works in the collection are dated 1960 or later. The avant-garde of such recent American movements as "pop," "op," hard edge and color painting are prominent, although many artists are represented by their prints.

Tom Wesselman, Roy Lichtenstein, Robert Indiana, Jim Dine, George Segal and Claes Oldenburg form a

Above: ANGEL OF DEATH by Leonard Baskin (1922-). Drawing, ink on paper. Death is probably Baskin's most persistent and most powerful theme. However, he sees it not as a tragic or maudlin event, but as an affirmation of life and considers his work to be in reality "healthily morbid." *The Washington Gallery of Modern Art.* Anonymous gift.

strong pop, or new realist, group. It has been said of Indiana (born Robert Clark, in 1928 in Indiana), as well as other pop artists, that they take "The world too seriously not to be amused by it." Indiana's "New York City," a 1962 work at the gallery, may support this, as well as the claim that pop art, unlike much of the art that immediately preceded it, accepts its environment as being neither good nor bad, only different.

Indiana, the most literary of the group, combines geometric clarity with poetry by including literature and history in his art. Literary and historical references, frequently those associated with lower Manhattan's former shipbuilding district are, at first glance, subordinated to geometry. On further observation, however, the literary and historical content comes to the fore.

Serigraphs by Richard Anuszkiewicz and Reginald

Neal are among the op offerings, while behind these a whole troup of established moderns includes Kenzo Okada, Harry Bertoia, Jack Tworkov, Morris Louis, David Park, Ellsworth Kelly and Robert Goodnough.

Still farther back in the short perspective of a decade of tumultuous development in American art are other abstract expressionists and a few such independents as Leonard Baskin and Walter Murch. Baskin (1922-), whose style and themes may seem somewhat anachronistic to some, is much admired for the brilliance of his drawing, the evocative power of his images and for his sincerity. His "Angel of Death" in the gallery's collection is perhaps less representational than most of his work, but is nonetheless powerful. Of death, probably his most persistent theme, he has said: "My work is really healthily morbid. I see death as an affirmation of life . . . not maudlin or tragic."

Some key figures in contemporary art missing from the 1966 catalogues are Stuart Davis, Hans Hofmann and Willem de Kooning, yet it can only be a matter of time until examples of their work are acquired. Similarly, sculpture holdings are bound to increase. Rudolf Hoflehner's spare, five-foot-high bronze "Figure," the

ruggedly dynamic bronze "Europa" by Ruben Nakian and Seymour Lipton's "Spinner" are among the half-dozen sculptures recently added to the collection.

By intention, much of the young museum's energy and substance has gone into temporary exhibitions and it has been generous in lending from its collection for such exhibitions elsewhere. Special one-man shows have brought to Washington the sculpture of David Smith, Anthony Caro and Reuben Nakian, a Franz Kline memorial exhibition in 1962, and exhibitions of painting by Morris Louis, Richard Diebenkorn, Ellsworth Kelly and others. At any time, visitors to the gallery are likely to find a new temporary exhibition to supplement the permanent displays.

So rapidly has it grown that The Washington Gallery of Modern Art felt the need for larger quarters before it was five years old, confirming the belief of the founding trustees that Washington would welcome a museum committed to presenting the best and most controversial 20th-century art.

The Washington Gallery of Modern Art: Washington, D. C. Open Tuesday through Saturday, 10 a.m. to 5 p.m.; Sun., 2 p.m. to 6 p.m. Closed Monday and legal holidays.

Left: FIGURE by Rudolf Hoflehner (1916-). Bronze. This former metallurgist turned naturally to sculpture in metals. *The Washington Gallery of Modern Art.* Gift of David Kreeger.

Below: NEW YORK CITY, 1962 by Robert Indiana (Robert Clark) (1928-). Oil. The "pop" artist refers to his home street, Coenties Slip, originally an inlet, now filled in. Gift of Mr. and Mrs. J. Eisenstein. *Washington Gallery of Modern Art.*

III SOUTH

THE ARKANSAS ARTS CENTER

A history-in-brief of America's progressive involvement in the arts may be traced in the growth of The Arkansas Arts Center in Little Rock — from a club to a collection, then to a small museum and now to a center for all the arts. Theater, dance, music, exhibitions, lectures, a school of art and drama, local and state-wide classes in arts and crafts for children and adults, traveling exhibits, an "artmobile" and a myriad of services and resources — such is the nature of an art center in the second half of the 20th century, taking The Arkansas Arts Center as a model.

For most of the half-century since the Little Rock Fine Arts Club first met in 1914 the art collection has been the hub of its activities. In 1927, prefiguring the state-encompassing arts center to come, the club reorganized as the Fine Arts Club of Arkansas and a year later opened Little Rock's first art museum, with an exhibit in the new Pulaski County Courthouse.

By mid-century standards growth was slow. In 1934, 20 years after the tentative beginnings, the club owned little more than 100 works of art. Yet even so, the need for more space was evident; and, with private gifts and government assistance, a museum building was erected on park lands. When the Museum of Fine Arts opened in 1937, the permanent collection of 200 pieces, together with the building, became city property and Little Rock assumed the cost of maintaining building and grounds.

Another 20 years passed as endowment and collections grew slowly. Then, in 1957, as a result of a Junior League Community Arts Council survey, a Community Center of Arts and Sciences was created, which soon joined forces with the Museum of Fine Arts. From this union, with state-wide support, came The Arkansas Arts Center, a remodeled museum with extensive new construction and an educational program that was in action even during building operations. Soon there developed all the complex ways and means of an art center serving the whole region.

The Fifth Delta Art Exhibition, showing art from the states in the Mississippi delta area, opened the remodeled galleries in 1963, to be followed by a distinguished program of temporary exhibitions. Meanwhile the center's artmobile, the gift of Mr. and Mrs. Winthrop Rockefeller, Mr. and Mrs. David Rockefeller and the Barton Foundation, began its tours throughout the state carrying selections from the permanent collection and special exhibits.

Gifts from Mr. and Mrs. F.W. Allsopp, who made the major private contributions to the original museum building fund, and from members of the Rockefeller family and many others, have built a collection of paintings, drawings, prints and sculpture favoring American art and modern European works. Among older works is "The Adoration of the Shepherds," by Francesco Bassano, the gift in 1939 of Samuel H. Kress.

A number of 18th- and 19th-century American paintings were given by the Allsopps in the 1930's, including portraits by John Hesselius, Gilbert Stuart and Charles B. King, landscapes by Asher B. Durand and Thomas Moran, John James Audubon's "Five Birds" and Frederic Remington's picture called "The Scout."

One of the major 20th-century paintings belonging to the Arts Center is the "Andromeda" by Odilon Redon, a work of 1912 that is a little less than six-by-three feet in size, picturing the daughter of Cepheus chained to the rock awaiting deliverance from the monster by Perseus. Andromeda is presented as a graceful standing figure in a formal composition overlaid with flowers.

Another important work is the large 77-by-64-inch oil,"Two Women," by Diego Rivera (1886-1957), painted in 1913-1914 during his long European sojourn at a time when he was close to the cubist movement. Following certain principles of early analytic cubism, the handsome canvas presents two readily distinguishable figures, reduced to configurations of planes that nonetheless respect the human form and proportions. The two women are placed in a curious architectural setting that seems to define a shallow interior space yet includes roof tops and other indications of a cityscape.

Rivera, perhaps best known for his murals, was a leader in the renaissance of Mexican art that followed the revolution of 1910. During his life his work sometimes aroused controversy on political grounds because of his leftist sympathies.

The arts center loan exhibition of 1964 that reviewed the surrealist art of the Belgian painter René Magritte was the occasion for the acquisition of a pen drawing made especially by the artist for the frontispiece of the exhibition catalogue. In this drawing a ponderous rock floats in mid-air above a landscape, a subject familiar from other works, to which the artist added a sleeping figure, possibly portraying himself, wrapped like a mummy and resting in a coffin-like box that fills the upper register of the picture.

The museum's print collection holds some important and rare examples, emphasizing contemporaries, including several etchings and a color aquatint by Pablo Picasso purchased by the arts center.

Among the works expressive of the support given to Arkansas artists are the watercolor and collage, "Horse," by Daniel K. Teis, and sculpture by Rodger A. Mack purchased from the highly successful annual Delta exhibitions.

The pattern of accelerating interest and activity in the arts that is evident in the development of The Arkansas Arts Center assures the residents of the state and visitors from afar that they will be rewarded by significant exhibitions, or drama, or music, or dance, in the normal program of the center.

Above: ANDROMEDA by Odilon Redon (1840-1916). Oil. Andromeda, chained and awaiting deliverance from the monster, is presented as a graceful figure in this formal composition overlaid with flowers, a major 20th-century work in the center. Gift of David Rockefeller. *The Arkansas Arts Center.*

Left: TWO WOMEN by Diego Rivera (1886-1957). Oil. This handsome 1914 canvas presents two figures, reduced to configurations of planes, which still respect human forms and proportions. The curious setting seems to be an interior, and yet it includes some indications of a cityscape. Gift of Abby Rockefeller Mause. *The Arkansas Arts Center.*

The Arkansas Arts Center: Little Rock, Ark. Open Tuesday through Saturday, 10 a.m. to 5 p.m.; Sunday and holidays, 12 p.m. to 5 p.m.

William E. Davis

BIRMINGHAM MUSEUM OF ART

Where two railroads crossed, the city of Birmingham was founded in 1872. It grew swiftly and still was very young as cities go when in 1950 a museum board was created by city ordinance to do something about art.

Since it was organized in 1908, the Birmingham Art Association had assiduously promoted art interests, including the idea of a city art museum, and that dream became fact in 1951, when the Birmingham Museum of Art was opened to the public in temporary quarters in City Hall.

A year later the initial exhibits were augmented significantly by the gift of more than 25 paintings from the Samuel H. Kress Foundation, stepping forward to aid yet another regional art center.

Still growing like Topsy, in 1959 the museum moved its collections into the newly constructed Oscar Wells Memorial, a specially designed museum building, up to date in every way, even to the wiring for telecasts from the galleries when more color television sets are in use. The Helen J. Wells bequest provided funds for the structure, named to honor her husband who had

been a leader in Birmingham, while the extent of public interest was made clear when the citizens voted funds to acquire the museum site.

The long-range Birmingham plan envisions expansion to double or triple the size of the museum, increasing the collections accordingly while raising standards of quality. By design, the museum displays to the best of its ability art of the entire world, from antiquity to the present, beginning with Paleolithic and Neolithic tools in the Rives Collection of Palestinian Art.

As might be expected, the holdings are limited in some areas, but the ambitious museum represents the Far East with modern Japanese and Chinese ceramics and textiles as well as with ancient bronzes and pottery. Classical antiquity, the Near East and Egypt are represented by small but growing collections, while for pre-Columbian art there are quite a few examples from Mexico, Middle America and Peru (including an outstanding collection of Chimú gold), and extensive holdings of objects from various parts of the United States.

European art, especially painting, is substantially exhibited with Italian, Dutch, Flemish and English examples, although 19th-century France and the modern period are represented largely through the collection of prints. While weak in the 18th and 19th centuries,

Right: CERES AND POMONA (The Horn of Plenty) by Peter Paul Rubens (1577-1640). Oil. At times Rubens tended to excess, as in this painting of two ample goddesses with an attendant, but few artists have been as popular and as famous. *Birmingham Museum of Art,* Birmingham, Alabama.

Below: SAINT BARTHOLOMEW by Perugino (Pietro Vannucci) (c. 1446-1523). Wood. Perugino, a master of the Umbrian School, has pictured the saint holding a knife symbolic of his martyrdom by being flayed alive. *Birmingham Museum of Art,* Birmingham, Alabama. Samuel H. Kress Collection.

A. C. Keily Studio

American art of the 20th century has been collected with many regional examples and some by nationally known artists.

A major strength of the Birmingham Museum of Art is the Kress Collection of Italian paintings, dating from the end of the 13th century to the end of the 18th, which the foundation enlarged by a second gift on the occasion of the opening of the new museum building.

Starting with a panel painting of "The Madonna and Child" with two saints, by a Tuscan artist from the last part of the 13th century, the Italian works range through many schools, ending with a "View of the Grand Canal, Venice" by Antonio Canaletto and several other 18th-century pictures.

Highlights of the Italian collection include the "Madonna and Child" attributed to Lorenzo Veneziano, with the lovely Madonna holding a pink rose; the sorrowful "Christ Showing the Symbols of the Passion," which is assigned to the Florentine Jacopo del Sellaio; a vigorously active "Allegory of Vigilance" by Jacopo Robusti Tintoretto; and "Landscape with Figures" by Alessandro Magnasco, a painting of the late 17th century in which tiny figures by the edge of a steam are overshadowed by the feathery trees.

An early 16th-century panel painting portrays "Saint Bartholomew" holding a knife, symbol of his martyrdom because he was flayed alive. It is the work of Perugino (born Pietro Vannucci), a master of the Umbrian School and a teacher of Raphael in Florence around 1500-1504. His portraits are noted for their simple charm.

When one of the museum's temporary exhibitions, "Dutch and Flemish Painting," was hung in the spring of 1966, eleven of the paintings and a tapestry were from the permanent collection. One was "The Battle of Pavia," a Kress Foundation gift, by an unknown Flemish artist, probably painted soon after the date of the battle in 1525. It is on a large panel, nearly six feet wide, with elaborately detailed figures, fortifications and landscape, recounting the defeat of the French and the capture of Francis I. Another was the painting of two ample nude goddesses with an attendant, the "Ceres and Pomona," also called "The Horn of Plenty" by Peter Paul Rubens.

The Birmingham Museum holds several special collections, among them the Lamprecht Collection of Iron Art loaned by the American Cast Iron Pipe Company. In 1966 its first annual exhibition of "Religion in Art" attracted national attention.

Birmingham Museum of Art: Birmingham, Ala. Open Mon. through Sat., 10 a.m. to 5 p.m.; Thurs., 10 a.m. to 9 p.m.; Sun., 2 p.m. to 6 p.m.

Below: THE BATTLE OF PAVIA. Flemish master (c. 1525). Oil on panel. This large painting commemorates the Battle of Pavia fought in 1525, which drove the French from the Duchy of Milan. Elaborate figures, fortifications and landscape recount the French defeat and capture of Francis I. *Birmingham Museum of Art*, Birmingham, Alabama. Samuel H. Kress Collection, 1955.

THE HIGH MUSEUM OF ART

As the Phoenix from the fire, so the Atlanta Memorial Cultural Center in Atlanta, Georgia, has risen from the ashes of the June 3, 1962, disaster at Orly airport, Paris, where many Atlantans perished, all members of the Atlanta Art Association. The new Atlanta Art Alliance, formed to operate the center, combines the Art Association, with its High Museum of Art and Atlanta School of Art, and the Atlanta Symphony, to bring under one roof the study, creation and enjoyment of the visual and performing arts.

In this grand plan for community cultural life, The High Museum of Art has a central role, exhibiting its permanent collection of European and American art, as well as some Oriental and pre-Columbian material, while engaged in museum-related educational projects.

It is an active museum; a graphic representation of its development would parallel that of many things in the 20th century, from institutions, to speed of travel, to population growth. Starting with a flat curve in the first decades of the century, the graph line turned sharply upward in the 1940's and 1950's and continues to rise at an unusually high rate.

Soon after the new century began, an organization was chartered to "promote interest in the fine and applied arts, to give lectures and practical instruction, and to found a museum and an art school" in Atlanta. Not until after 1926 did the art association find permanent quarters, when Mrs. Joseph M. High gave her home for use as a museum and art school. The museum began functioning two years later when its first professional museum director was appointed.

Visitors to the High Museum find a substantial collection of American painting from the 18th to the 20th centuries, impressive Italian Renaissance painting and northern European sculpture, some 19th-century French painting and prints and drawings that range from the 16th century to modern times, with great strength in the contemporary era.

The J.J. Haverty Collection of European and American Art, the Kress Collection, the Memory Lane Gallery and Collection for memorial gifts of art from many periods, the Ralph K. Uhrey print collection and several funds for acquisition, have made possible the concentration of fine works of art that make the High Museum supreme in its region.

The collections of early art were much enhanced when, in 1958, the Samuel H. Kress Foundation gift added major examples of Italian and northern European painting and sculpture. One of the earliest pieces is the mid-14th-century tempera painting on a wooden panel,

Above: SAINT CATHERINE OF ALEXANDRIA. Siena (14th century). Tempera on panel. The saint carries a palm leaf symbolizing her victory in martyrdom. *The High Museum of Art,* Atlanta, Georgia. Samuel H. Kress Collection, 1957.

a half-length "St. Catherine of Alexandria" holding a palm leaf. The unknown Sienese artist united the Byzantine interest in decorative pattern and richly ornamented surfaces with the then new naturalism and concern for human qualities in depicting the saint. The painting of "St. Vitalis," also in the museum's Kress Collection, may be from the same dismembered altarpiece.

Another great painting in the Kress Collection gift is the "Madonna and Child," by Giovanni Bellini (c. 1340-1516) and dated about 1512. Bellini stands as a link between the early and high Renaissance. His works range from paintings which are sculptural and precise in the medieval spirit to later works suffused with the mellow light and color of Venetian taste, such as this Madonna. Trained by his father, Jacopo Bellini, he also came under influence of his brother-in-law, Andrea Mantegna, who was in the forefront of the revival of

Above: MADONNA AND CHILD by Giovanni Bellini (c. 1340-1516). Oil on panel. Painted in the artist's later years, this Madonna is suffused with the mellow light of Venetian taste. *The High Museum of Art,* Atlanta, Georgia. Samuel H. Kress Collection, 1958.

classical sculpture and architecture. Bellini and his famous pupils, Giorgione da Castelfranco and Titian, brought Renaissance Venetian painting to its pinnacle.

This Madonna was done when Bellini was in his eighties. He enlivened the static frontal pose of the Madonna through the active turning of the figure of the Child to the viewer's left, which is offset by the zigzag formation of the landscape on the right, leading into the distance.

An important "Crucifixion" by Annibale Carracci, the portrait of a youth by Michelangelo Amerighi da Caravaggio, and the oval "Offering by Young Vestal Priestesses to Juno Lucina" by Giovanni Battista Tiepolo, also are in the Kress Collection, as is the 40-inch-high "St. Andrew, the Apostle" carved in lindenwood, by Tilman Riemenschneider and dated about 1504-1505.

More Italian, German, Dutch and Flemish works entered the High Museum by purchase and as gifts from individual donors following the arrival of the Kress pictures. One of these is the "Games on Ice" by the Dutch painter Barent Avercamp, a small 10 3/4-by-17 7/16-inch oil on panel, its lower half peopled by the slanting figures of skaters and showing a great many ways of getting about on ice. Another, even smaller, is a fascinating picture of nightmare fantasies in the manner of Hieronymus Bosch, "The Temptation of St. Anthony" by Herri Met de Bles.

French painting is handsomely represented by the 1903 "Houses of Parliament" by Claude Monet; a brilliant landscape by Louis Eugène Boudin; the romantic "Garden Fête" by Adolphe Joseph Monticelli, whose fresh way of fragmenting brilliant color is better understood by the public today than when he painted; and canvases by Gustave Courbet, Jean Baptiste Camille Corot and Eugène Fromentin.

The museum is fortunate in owning the "Italian Landscape" by the English artist Richard Wilson, who on a trip to Italy abandoned portraiture for landscape painting.

Above: PORTRAIT OF ELIZABETH DEERING WENTWORTH by John Singleton Copley (1738-1815). Oil. Copley's early portraits reflect a direct and probing approach. *The High Museum of Art,* Atlanta, Georgia. Henry B. Scott Purchase, 1959.

Above: THE CRUCIFIXION by Annibale Carracci (1560-1609). A man and boy dressed in clothes of the artist's time add immediacy to the Agony on the Cross. *The High Museum of Art,* Atlanta, Georgia. Samuel H. Kress Collection, 1955.

Beginning with John Singleton Copley's sensitive and winning "Portrait of Elizabeth Deering Wentworth," painted about 1765, there are portraits by Americans including Thomas Sully's thoughtful "Reverend George Houston Woodough" and Charles Willson Peale's strong likeness of Senator William R. Crawford of Georgia.

Members of the Hudson River School are represented, and also "The Eight." One of the latter, Arthur B. Davies, who was a leader in organizing the famed Armory Show of 1913 which introduced modern European art to America, was far from being typical of the Ashcan School in his own poetic work. The High Museum's painting by Davies, called "Air, Light, and Waves," is an ethereal vision of nudes in a vaporous environment.

Another member of "The Eight" was William Glackens (1870-1938), whose "Still Life With Roses and Fruit" (p. 87) is one of the most attractive pieces in the High Museum. Glackens was a superb draftsman, but in early work his colors were somber. Later, however, he adopted the gay, sun-warmed colors seen in this still life and lost the strength of his earlier paintings.

Several of the great American individuals can be studied in good examples of their work. A *trompe-l'oeil* still life by William M. Harnett, an eerie, rhythmic, near-abstraction of trees and buildings by Charles Burchfield called "Midnight" and John Marin's watercolor of dancing waves are among them.

The admirable American collection continues into the 1960's with the work of established avant-garde artists.

A prime example of contemporary sculpture is the 14-inch-high carving in beechwood by Henry Moore (1898-) called "Composition." Moore has been a student of medieval and primitive sculpture but this piece runs parallel to the bromorphism in work by Constantin Brancusi, Pablo Picasso and Jean Arp. Although dated 1932, early in the sculptor's career, "Composition" is consistent with much later work in being highly tactile, smoothed and clearly shaped, with strong suggestions of organic forms. Some idea of the meaning behind these rounded forms can be derived from a statement of Moore's: "The meaning and significance of form itself probably depends on the countless associations of man's history. For example, rounded forms convey an idea of fruitfulness, maturity, probably because the earth, women's breasts and most fruits are rounded...."

Another contemporary work, the bronze "Tragic Flight" by Virginio Ferrari, is a memorial to the Atlanta Art Association members whose plane crashed at Orly.

The High Museum of Art: Atlanta, Ga. Open Monday through Friday, 5 p.m. to 10 p.m.; Saturday, 10 a.m. to 5 p.m.; Sunday, 1 p.m. to 5 p.m.

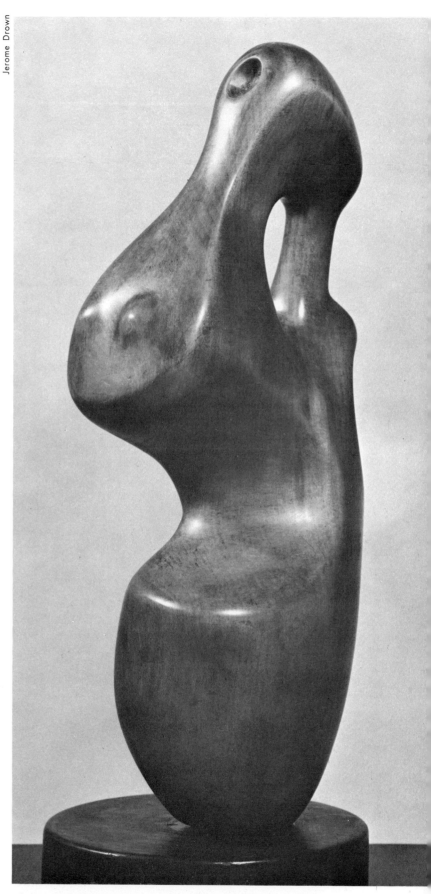

Jerome Drown

Above: COMPOSITION by Henry Moore (1898-). Beechwood. Highly tactile, smoothed and clearly shaped, Moore's carving has strong suggestions of organic forms. *The High Museum of Art*, Atlanta, Georgia. Gift of Rich's Inc., 1952.

ISAAC DELGADO
MUSEUM OF ART

Like a sleeping giant unaware of latent powers, the Isaac Delgado Museum of Art, dedicated in 1911, awoke in 1953 when the Kress Collection arrived on extended loan, and in 1965 rose and flexed its muscles "to bring Estelle home." Estelle Musson, Mme. René de Gas, was the subject of "Portrait of Estelle," painted in 1872 by Edgar Degas while in New Orleans on a four-month visit, and it was the painted Estelle that New Orleanians brought home after raising nearly $200,000 to purchase it. This was an astonishing sum for one picture in a museum that had existed for more than 40 years, with a total endowment of $75,000, yielding less than $5,000 annually, all earmarked for special projects.

When the sugar magnate Isaac Delgado gave New Orleans funds to build the museum, it had no endowment and only the hope that gifts would build a collection. The initial gifts included Chinese jades from the Morgan Whitney Collection, the Harrod Collection of silver, the Alvin P. Howard Collection of Greek vases and ancient glass and, in 1914, the Mr. and Mrs. Chapman H. Hyams Collection of Salon and Barbizon paintings.

For the next three decades the institution was more an art center than a museum of art, dependent upon temporary shows to eke out its exhibition program.

Then, after World War II, came gifts of painting and sculpture, many of the 18th and 19th centuries. The Kress Collection added examples from the 13th to the 18th centuries, and in recent years there have been many gifts of European and American 20th-century art. It took an effort to reinstall the museum's most important holdings, undertaken in the early 1960's, to reveal how little space was available after devoting three galleries to the Kress Collection and one to the Hyams Collection.

The mid-century American impetus to collect art was accelerated in New Orleans by the Delgado Museum

Below: PORTRAIT OF ESTELLE by Edgar Degas (1834-1917). Oil. Painted in New Orleans in 1872, the artist's feeling for the isolation of the blind girl is revealed in a sensitive composition returned to the city in 1965. *Isaac Delgado Museum of Art.*

policy of presenting temporary exhibitions of high quality, borrowed from collectors and dealers, to show something of what has been acquired by individuals and what remains available. Thanks to a positive presentation of museum needs, the gifts of art poured in, amounting, in 1964 alone, to more than $500,000 in value, many of them purchased specifically for the museum. The City of New Orleans — which provides for salaries, some operating costs and a small acquisition fund — recently pledged a new $1,800,000 wing.

The sleeping museum has fully wakened and Isaac Delgado's conception now holds in reverse: Instead of a new museum building attracting gifts of art, the influx of gifts now demands expansion of facilities.

The Hyams Collection, consisting of works of the Barbizon School of landscapists and other 19th-century artists, celebrated its Golden Anniversary in 1964 with a newly decorated room and reissue of its catalogue which includes contemporaries. Considered an outstanding collection of masterworks when it was presented in 1964, the Hyams Collection survived the official art world's deprecation in the second quarter of the century, and in the third quarter can be re-evaluated with sufficient detachment to recognize the painters' merits. Needless to add, Adolphe William Bouguereau's "Whisperings of Love" with its chaste maiden listening to winged cupid at her ear; Alma-Tadema's cool and luscious "Shrine of Venus," a picture of beautiful women awaiting their turn in the marble foyer of a hairdresser's shop; and Carl Kronberger's 7¼-by-5⅜-inch oil on wood panel, a photographic likeness called "Head of Old Woman," have been favorites of the public at all times.

The usual four-century range of the Samuel H. Kress Collection provides the Delgado Museum with a good survey of Italian painting, from the small early lindenwood panel, "The Last Supper," with its now charming primitive perspective, to Giovanni Battista Tiepolo's "Portrait of a Boy Holding a Book" and a studio version of his picture, "The Minuet," one of a pair of carnival scenes now in the Louvre.

"Saint Paul" by Vincenzo Foppa; the "Saint Sebastian" by Giuliano Bugiardini; Bernardino Luini's "Adoration of the Christ Child"; and Lorenzo Lotto's dignified "Portrait of a Bearded Man," his beard red and his vest purple, are of primary interest. Other notable paintings are the "Sacra Conversazione" by Veronese, with St. Agnes kneeling before the Virgin and Child, and two pictures in which wild moods of nature are the true subjects — the "Landscape with Soldiers in a Ravine" by Salvator Rosa, and the tumultuous "Seascape with Friars" by Alessandro Magnasco.

Surprises await the visitor in the Delgado Museum's recent acquisitions by gift and purchase. There are two

Above: HEAD OF A PRINCESS. Nigeria, Benin (17th century). Bronze. *Isaac Delgado Museum of Art.* Anonymous gift.

Below: OEUVRE CINÉTIQUE—INSTABILITÉ by Julio Le Parc. The 13-inch high wood construction hangs perpendicular to the museum wall and has a light source beneath. The light reflects off the highly polished chrome surfaces of the disc, as light is reflected from a child's wading pool. *Isaac Delgado Museum of Art.* Gift of Mrs. Edgar B. Stern.

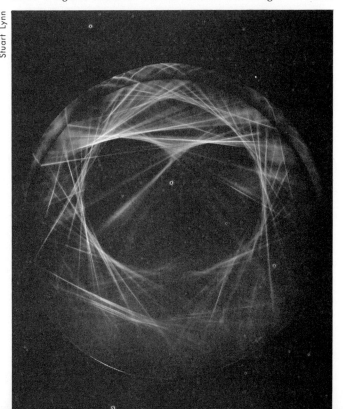

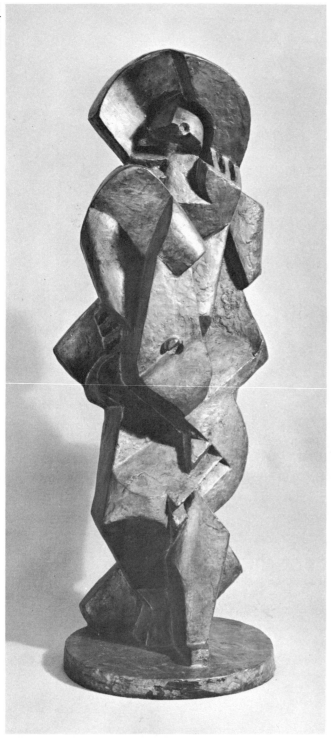

Above: THE BATHER by Jacques Lipschitz (1891-   ) Bronze with gilt wash. Interlocking slabs form a work viewable from many angles. *Isaac Delgado Museum of Art.* Anonymous gift.

Above: THE GAUGUIN DOORS by Paul Gauguin (1848-1903). Oil on glass. These two unique doors, dated 1893, were executed for the artist's Tahitian cottage. *Isaac Delgado Museum of Art.* M. Knoedler and anonymous donors purchase, 1964.

unique painted-glass doors by Paul Gauguin, executed for his Tahitian cottage and dated 1893, which were purchased in 1964. "The Battle of New Orleans" by Hyacinthe de La Clotte, painted in 1815, is an elaborately detailed overview of the field of battle on which the combatants are marshaled like toy soldiers, given in 1965.

The locally celebrated "Portrait of Estelle" by Edgar Degas (1834-1917), caught the imagination of New Orleanians in part because the artist painted the

picture while in the city from October 28, 1872, to March 4, 1873, and in part because Estelle Musson, who married the artist's brother René, was born in New Orleans. Acquisition of the painting was the occasion for a major Degas exhibition at the Delgado Museum in 1965, an assemblage of paintings and drawings connected with Degas' visit and portraits of New Orleanians he painted in Europe.

The likeness of the 29-year-old Estelle shows her

(Continued on page 91)

Southern Museums

Above: PUMA. Peru, Mochica. (400-1000 A.D.). Hammered gold. The Mochica, which is a truly regional style, is bold and dynamic, showing a highly developed sculptural tradition. The *Virginia Museum of Fine Arts*. The Glasgow Fund, 1959.

Below: STILL LIFE WITH ROSES AND FRUIT by William Glackens (1870-1938). Oil. Influenced by Renoir's impressionistic style and use of warm, sharp colors, Glackens brought a new freshness to the world of American art. *High Museum of Art*.

Below: THE MEETING OF ABRAHAM AND MELCHIZEDECK by Peter Paul Rubens (1577-1640). Oil. Rubens designed his magnificent paintings in terms of light and color. Here history and allegory flow together in his depiction of Abraham's sharing of bread and wine with Melchizedeck, the King of Salem. *John and Mable Ringling Museum of Art.*

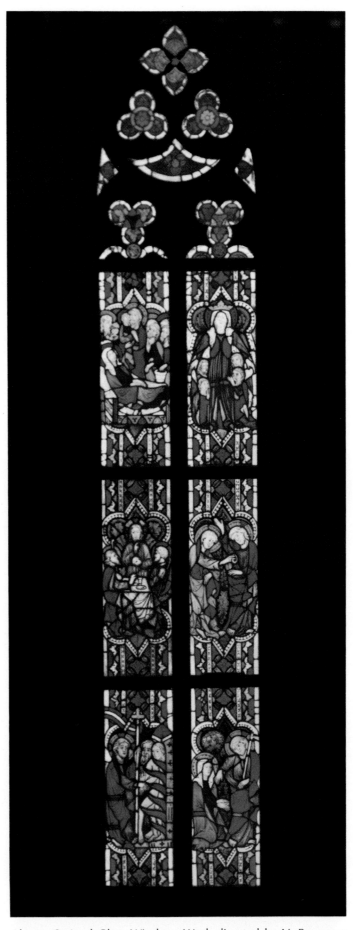

Above: Stained-Glass Window. Work directed by V. Berenger. Austria. (14th century). The translucent brilliance of stained glass added pictorial richness to the interiors of medieval Gothic churches. *The Virginia Museum of Fine Arts*. The Williams Fund.

Right: JEANNE AND LYDIA by Eugene Speicher (1883-   ). Oil. As a leading American portraitist, Speicher achieved a rare, warm blending of the physical and spiritual components inherent in his subjects. *Isaac Delgado Museum*. Gift of Mrs. E. A. Schaefer.

Below: ACHILLES ON SKYROS by Nicolas Poussin (1594-1665). Oil. Poussin's admiring study of ancient statuary and Greco-Roman tradition is evident in the origins of this classical work. *The Virginia Museum of Fine Arts*. The Glasgow Fund, 1957.

(Continued from page 86)

standing at the end of a long table, arranging flowers in a vase. At that time she could only feel and smell the flowers, for she was blinded by ophthalmia six years before, and the artist's sense for her isolation is revealed in the composition. Degas' letters revealed his admiration for her ability to move about the house unaided.

She stands left of center, a window filling the right upper part of the picture, and the drawing of her figure indicates with restraint her pregnancy with the third child to be born to René. Around her, the painting is left unfinished as a world of shadows, quite complete in itself, although after Degas' death in 1917 the canvas was found with additions at top and bottom indicating that he had considered enlarging the composition.

Other recent acquisitions range through Far and Near Eastern art; pre-Columbian art; a Constable landscape; a double-portrait, "Jeanne and Lydia" (p. 90), by Eugene Speicher, the 20th-century American artist noted for his depiction of women; serigraphs and three paintings by Victor Vasarely, famous French "op" artist; a canvas by the Belgian surrealist René Magritte; paintings by Odilon Redon, Maurice Utrillo, Wassily Kandinsky and Joan Miró; and a number of contemporary American works. Sculpture that has entered the collection recently includes bronzes by Auguste Rodin

and Degas, an early piece by Jacques Lipchitz, a bronze construction by David Hare, nine bronze reliefs executed by Jean Arp, a space construction by Naum Gabo and Julio Le Parc's "Oeuvre Cinétique — Instabilité," a grand prize winner of the Venice Biennale.

Isaac Delgado Museum of Art: New Orleans, Louisiana. Open Tuesday through Saturday, 10 a.m. to 5 p.m.; Sunday, 1 p.m. to 6 p.m. Closed Monday and national holidays.

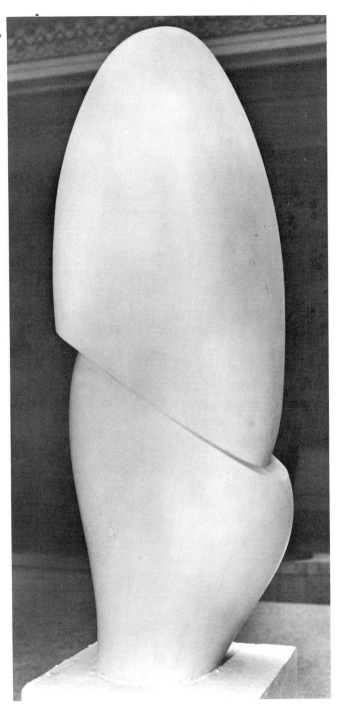

C. J. Loughlin

Above: TOILET OF PSYCHE by Charles Natoire (1700-1777). Oil. The beautiful goddess is surrounded by handmaidens. *Isaac Delgado Museum of Art.* Bequest of Charles F. Claiborne.

Above: COUPÉS SUPERPOSÉES by Hans Jean Arp (1887-1966). Marble. Arp's curving contours are derived from natural forms. *Isaac Delgado Museum of Art.* Gift of Mrs. Edgar Stern.

JOHN AND MABLE RINGLING
MUSEUM OF ART

"Flamboyance" and "spectacle" are words that leap to mind in connection with the name John Ringling, linked as it is to the American circus, with all its expansive color and glamor. Yet when Ringling decided to create a museum he did not think of a museum of the circus; that was left for his heir, the State of Florida, to accomplish in recognition that an important part of American life might otherwise soon be lost.

John and Mable Ringling had seen the museums of Europe, and it was a museum of art that they envisioned when they determined to complement their palatial Venetian-style residence on the shores of Sarasota Bay with a splendid building to house the Renaissance and Baroque paintings they most enjoyed.

There is something of the flamboyant in Baroque art, particularly in that of Peter Paul Rubens whose work was a touchstone for Ringling, and spectacle, in the classic sense of the term, was never far from the Ringlings' thoughts when house and gardens and museum were planned. What they built, however, was done with devotion to their taste for the resplendent and the grand.

Their home, "Ca'd'Zan," Venetian dialect for "House of John," recalls the Palace of the Doges in the design of its bayside façade. The Italian Renaissance style of the structure that houses the works of art brought lasting dignity to the estate built on drained swampland. Ringling had purchased the tract in 1912 and built his mansion and the museum in the late 1920's, the John and Mable Ringling Museum of Art opening in 1930.

The U-shaped museum building encloses a garden court in the Italian manner. Its loggiaed wings contain a miscellany of archeological objects purchased when the Gréau and Cesnola collections were sold by the Metropolitan Museum in 1928, and also some examples of Indian Gandharan sculpture. Scattered through the court and elsewhere on the grounds are reproductions of classical and Renaissance sculptures, the largest of which is a bronze copy of Michalangelo's "David" that stands above a pool at the west end of the court.

Early in 1967, a new wing was opened, extending one side of the court in harmonious architectural style. It added one-third more space and testified to the vitality of the growing museum.

As long as he could, after the museum opened in 1930, Ringling added to the collection, using his last available resources, even in the depth of the depression years. He knew that not all of the works of art he had gathered were up to the highest standards and he may have planned to remedy this as soon as finances allowed.

His death in 1936 ended these hopes, but the museum, its collections and the rest of the Ringling estate and fortune were left to the State of Florida. After a decade of litigation over the estate, the museum reopened as a public institution in 1946 and prospered under public administration in the hands of professional directors, the first of whom was A. Everett Austin, Jr., once director of the Wadsworth Atheneum in Hartford.

It was Austin who made the Ringling picture gallery into a museum of art and added wisely to the collections. In 1947 he opened the Ringling residence to the public as a historic house documenting the opulence of the 1920's; he started the Circus Museum in 1948; and in 1949 he acquired the internal structure of the 18th-century theater, originally built for the great hall of the castle of Catherine Cornaro at Asolo, near Venice. The State of Florida paid for the purchase, and by 1957 it was permanently installed and in use in a specially designed building near the art museum. It is equipped with 18th-century furniture, paintings and decorative objects and is unique in the Western Hemisphere.

As one of the country's leading experts on Baroque

Above: THE ARCHDUKE FERDINAND by Peter Paul Rubens (1577-1640). Oil. Gentleman and warrior become an allegory of war and peace. *John and Mable Ringling Museum of Art.*

Below: REST ON THE FLIGHT INTO EGYPT by Veronese (Paolo Caliari) (1528-1588). Oil. Magnificent in style, yet intimate in mood is the artist's portrayal of the Holy Family surrounded by angels. *John and Mable Ringling Museum of Art.*

art, Austin was the right man to prepare the Ringling collection for public exhibition and to strengthen it through purchases. The most impressive gallery in the museum is the one containing four of the 11 large paintings by Rubens (1577-1640), prepared as full-scale cartoons for tapestries that were to be woven by the Brussels weavers. The pictures were ordered about 1625 by the Infanta Isabella Clara Eugenia, then Governess of the Netherlands, who gave Rubens a handful of pearls in partial payment for his work.

The largest of the cartoons (p. 88) depicts a passage from *Genesis* which tells of the meeting of Abraham and Melchizedek, when the King of Salem offered the patriarch bread and wine, later to become symbols of the sacrament. Two other cartoons are in France, while the other five are lost. Painted by Rubens and assistants, the cartoons convey the full flavor of Baroque art, its heroic scale, opulent color and dynamic composition.

Peter Paul Rubens, called "Painter of Kings and King of Painters," was one of the most versatile figures in the history of art. Court painter, diplomat, connoisseur and classical scholar, he moved easily through the most exalted circles of late 16th-century and early 17th-century Europe. Yet he remained profoundly attached to his native Flanders. As the crowned heads of Europe showered commissions upon him, Rubens' large art studio, which included the notable Anthony van Dyck among the assistants, became the busiest in Europe.

The number of paintings by Rubens in the Ringling Museum, including the important "Departure of Lot and His Family from Sodom" and the portrait of "The Archduke Ferdinand," make this the largest collection of major works by Rubens in the United States.

With all its focus on the Baroque, the Ringling

Below: THE RAPE OF THE SABINE WOMEN by Jan Steen (1626-1679). Oil. Steen specialized in portraying groups of people in lively action. Here he adds a touch of humor to a usually serious subject by historically disguising the sly and rowdy Dutch peasants he always painted, placing them in a setting taken from the legends of Rome. *John and Mable Ringling Museum of Art.*

Museum pictures range from the late 14th to the end of the 18th century and recently have been extended to the 20th century.

One of the earliest is a Florentine School panel, "The Virgin and Child Adored by Angels," attributed to Mariotto di Nardo. "The Building of a Villa," with its foreground filled with construction workers at their various tasks, gave Piero di Cosimo ample scope to demonstrate the laws of linear perspective.

Paintings of the Baroque period include Bernardo Strozzi's impressive "Giving Drink to the Thirsty"; "Stormy Sea" by another Genoese, Alessandro Magnasco; one of the few works in America by Pietro da Cortona, "Hagar in the Wilderness," showing Lot's thirsty wife with an angel revealing to her a spring of water; and four paintings by Salvator Rosa, who anticipated the 19th-century's romantic approach to nature.

One important sculpture is the fresh and lively *bozzetto* by Giovanni Lorenzo Bernini, a sketch in clay

of an angel, acquired in 1960 through the Ringling endowment fund.

Apart from Rubens, northern European painting is significantly represented by works attributed to some of the greatest artists — Lucas Cranach, Rembrandt van Rijn and Frans Hals. One curious canvas is "The Rape of the Sabine Women" by Jan Steen, a turbulent scene of figures in a landscape in which Steen's typical Dutch peasants give a humorous interpretation of the classical story, including a damsel halfway up a tree yet caught by one leg by her pursuer.

Spanish and French painting is represented also by pictures to which are attached the names of El Greco, Jusepe de Ribera, Bartholomé Esteban Murillo, Velásquez and Nicolas Poussin. The largest known painting by Thomas Gainsborough, the "Equestrian Portrait of General Philip Honywood," another equestrian portrait by Sir Joshua Reynolds and portraits by Sir Henry Raeburn, stand among English paintings and lead into the 19th century.

A collection of drawings and prints is being formed. The library is being developed with the aim of making the Ringling Museum a major center of Baroque studies. The building also houses two permanent collections of faience, one of Dutch Delft and the other of 16th- to 19th-century European pottery.

John and Mable Ringling Museum of Art: Sarasota, Florida. Open Monday through Saturday, 9 a.m. to 5 p.m.; Sunday, 1 p.m. to 5 p.m. Closed Thanksgiving and Christmas.

Above: CARDINAL ALBRECHT AS SAINT JEROME by Lucas Cranach the Elder (1472-1553). Oil. A broadening perspective from the Cardinal's tiny figure reaches to symbolic animals in the foreground. *John and Mable Ringling Museum of Art.*

Above: A towering bronze cast of Michelangelo's "David," made especially for the Ringlings in Naples, Italy, stands high above a pool in the west end of the great central courtyard at the John and Mable Ringling Museum of Art.

THE NORTH CAROLINA MUSEUM OF ART

In some parts of the world it is not unusual for the state government to provide direct support for the arts through stipends for artists and subsidies for museums and festivals. In the United States, however, until quite recently, such government aid has been very rare, so rare that North Carolina can boast of being the first state in the union to devote public funds to the purchase of painting and sculpture. This money, not just for buildings and staff, but for works of art, is an investment that is certain to pay dividends in every way, from public education to monetary increment.

In less than 25 years the acorn grew into a mighty oak, from an idea in 1943 to a collection of more than 2,000 works of art.

The $1,000,000 appropriated by the North Carolina General Assembly in 1947 was conditional: The North Carolina State Art Society was required to find an equal amount. A pledge from the Samuel H. Kress Foundation to give painting and sculpture worth at least $1,000,000 met the first condition.

By the time The North Carolina Museum of Art opened on April 6, 1956, in a four-story building transformed into a modern museum by the state, the original collection had grown so much through gifts and bequests that the Kress Foundation more than doubled its contributions. In size and importance, North Carolina's Kress Collection is second only to the Kress collection in the National Gallery of Art.

Italian, Dutch, Flemish, French, German, Spanish, English and American paintings, together with sculpture and decorative arts, fill 56 galleries, arranged in historical sequence.

The Kress pictures occupy the main part of the first floor. More Flemish, Dutch, Italian and Spanish works fill 24 second-floor galleries; 17th-, 18th- and 19th-century French, English and American works are on the third floor; and on the fourth there is one large gallery and three smaller ones given to temporary and special exhibitions, with limited space for North Carolina art and for contemporary art, the department in which the museum is somewhat weak.

So large and inviting a collection can only be sketchily described, but a few of the greatest treasures may suggest the attractions that draw over 80,000 visitors annually.

True rarities are the great altarpiece by Giotto and his assistants; the painting, "St. Jerome Punishing the Heretic Sabinian," by Raphael, an artist who is represented in only four American museums; and the bronze figure of "Neptune" by Benvenuto Cellini — three

Below: SAINT JEROME PUNISHING THE HERETIC SABINIAN by Raphael (1483-1520). Oil. Here can be seen the flowing curves and balance of tension which are basic to Raphael's search for perfect form. Courtesy of *The North Carolina Museum of Art.*

artists whose works tell much about the Renaissance and its origins.

Giotto (c. 1266-1337) was one of the greatest painters of his time, and a progenitor of the Florentine School. His work unites the strong influence of northern Gothic art with something of Cimabue's Greek manner and the classical sculpture and mural decoration that he found in Rome. Typically simple in form, the museum's altarpiece displays Giotto's genius for conveying human expression with an economy of means that forecasts later achievements in the Renaissance. Depicting sacred personages with humanizing warmth was one of his great contributions.

The altarpiece is thought to have been painted for the Peruzzi Chapel in the Church of Santa Croce, Florence, about 1322. The central panel of the polyptych presents Christ with hand upraised in blessing and is attributed to Giotto. The side panels by assistants show the Virgin and St. John the Baptist flanking Christ, with St. John the Evangelist and St. Francis on the end panels. The five, from private collections, were brought together for the first time in centuries by the Kress purchases.

In the work of Raphael (1483-1520), the Renaissance reached a remarkable synthesis of styles. The powerful forms and expression of vigorous muscular action that characterize the work of Michelangelo; and the gentler, more lyrical subtleties of tonality and modeling found in Leonardo da Vinci's painting are transformed in a distinctive fashion in Raphael's work. These and other qualities are found in his flowing figural compositions, such as "St. Jerome," and in his objective, realistic portraits.

Cellini (1500-1571), who was 17 years younger than Raphael, was a fine goldsmith and a writer, as well as a sculptor. In this he epitomizes the diversity of the Renaissance spirit in Italy. His career was tumultuous, but the strength and originality of his work, such as "Neptune," have placed him among the great sculptors.

"The Adoration of the Child," a tondo panel by Sandro Botticelli; "Leda and the Swan," a composition by Il Sodoma derived from a design by Leonardo da Vinci; Veronese's "Baptism of Christ"; and Rembrandt van Rijn's handsome portrait, "Young Man with a Sword," are other works of special interest.

The list of artists represented in the museum reads like a history of Western art. The American Hudson River School of the 19th century is represented well; works by 20th-century German expressionists form an impressive group; the Spanish still-life collection is strong; and paintings by prominent mid-century Americans are also in the collection. Perhaps the only real hiatus in museum acquisitions is in late 19th- and early 20th-century French painting, not an easy gap to close.

Above: NEPTUNE by Benvenuto Cellini (1500-1571). Bronze. Cellini, also a writer and goldsmith, typified the true Renaissance spirit. Courtesy of *The North Carolina Museum of Art*.

The North Carolina Museum of Art: Raleigh, N. C. Open Tuesday through Saturday, 10 a.m. to 5 p.m.; Sunday, 2 p.m. to 6 p.m. Closed Monday, Thanksgiving, state Christmas holidays, and New Year's Day.

THE VIRGINIA MUSEUM
OF FINE ARTS

One sign that a museum of art has come of age is the publication of a catalogue of its collection — for such an undertaking is not begun casually, involving as it does the moments of truth when the author and the museum must face up to what each work really is and set down the facts as they are known.

The Virginia Museum of Fine Arts in Richmond was just 30 years old when it published its first major catalogue in 1966, "European Art in the Virginia Museum of Fine Arts," which described some 287 examples of painting, sculpture and decorative arts and listed others of its holdings. Previously, only the handbook of the Pratt Collection of Russian Imperial Jewels had been published; subsequent catalogues of ancient and Oriental art and of American art are projected.

In claiming to be so young, the museum does not forget that it has a venerable ancestry. The state of Washington and Jefferson has a long history of concern for the arts, perhaps most clearly expressed to modern eyes through the State Capitol Building, designed by Thomas Jefferson about 1785. In 1786 Richmond became the home of the Academy of Arts and Sciences of America, established by Louis XVI and the first of its kind in the New World.

Unfortunately, the academy withered after its prosperous years in the early 19th century and the arts were somewhat neglected until the 20th century. It was, however, a revival of the old Academy, named the Richmond Academy of Arts, that aided in bringing about, in 1936, the first state institution of the nation, The Virginia Museum of Fine Arts.

Earlier, in 1919, Judge John Barton Payne gave his collection of over 50 paintings to the state, and the pictures hung for years in Battle Abbey. Around 1930 Judge Payne offered $100,000, to be matched by the state, for construction of an art museum, and in 1934 the General Assembly created a Board of Trustees and assumed the costs of maintenance and salaries for the museum. Despite the depression, the matching money was found through private efforts, since the state could not provide it; and aided by a 30 per cent W.P.A. grant, the museum was opened in 1936, the first major art museum in the South. It was intended, in the dedicatory words of Governor Peery, "to foster the love, progress and understanding of art and beauty for the people of the state."

With the support of succeeding governors, this is just what the Virginia Museum has accomplished. It has carried art exhibits to all parts of the state with its famed pioneer "artmobiles," has befriended and engendered art groups everywhere in Virginia, and reaches out to communities smaller than Richmond through boxed exhibits, films, film strips, slides, art kits and traveling theatre presentations.

While communities and statewide activities grew from the beginning, the galleries of the museum had little to show except loan exhibitions until 1947, when the amazing T. Catesby Jones Collection of 20th-century art and the equally remarkable Lillian Thomas Pratt Collection of Russian Imperial Jewels came as bequests. Physical expansion of the museum in 1955 and 1956 was paralleled by the museum's greatest gift of works of art and endowment, the bequests of Mr. and Mrs. A. D. Williams of Richmond, and Mr. and Mrs. Arthur Glasgow, formerly of Richmond. By 1965 the museum had grown to the point where plans matured for two more wings to be built north and south of the existing structure.

The only American painting in the Williams bequest was one of Gilbert Stuart's popular portraits of George Washington. The rest of the extensive collection ranges from the 14th to the 19th centuries. Among early paintings purchased with income from the Williams and Glasgow endowments, the Venetian School

Below: PORTRAIT OF SASKIA VAN UYLENBORCH by Rembrandt van Rijn (1606-1669). Oil on panel. The portrait is of the artist's wife, done nine years before her death. *The Virginia Museum of Fine Arts.* Gift of Mrs. A. D. Williams.

Above: BRANCH HILL POND, HAMPSTEAD HEATH by John Constable (1776-1837). Oil. Constable in the "return to nature" theme of his landscapes, followed Wordsworthian Romanticism. *The Virginia Museum of Fine Arts.* Gift of Mrs. A. D. Williams.

diptych with "Eight Scenes from the Life of Christ" and the triptych of the "Crucifixion and Four Saints" by the Veronese painter Altichiero Altichieri, both 14th century, are of particular interest.

"The Death of Regulus," a dark, five-by-seven-foot composition of figures in a landscape witnessing the martyrdom of the Roman consul, is considered probably the most important work in the United States by the 17th-century Neopolitan artist, Salvator Rosa. Other notable Italian pictures are "The Assumption of Christ" by Giovanni Battista Tiepolo and "Piazza San Marco" by Francesco Guardi.

Peter Paul Rubens is represented by the sympathetic portrait of his second wife, Hélène Fourment, thought to be the original study for a large group portrait of the artist with his wife and small child, but disputed because there are four other versions; and by a small, vigorously brushed sketch for one of a series of decorations ordered in 1636 by Philip IV of Spain. The sketch, titled "Pallas and Arachne," recounts the dispute over skill in weaving between the Lydian maiden and Athena that ended when the goddess saved the despairing Arachne's life but changed her into a spider.

A lively "Dance of the Peasants' by David Teniers the Younger, showing a long line of figures frozen in perpetual motion; the "Portrait of a Young Woman" of serious mien by Rembrandt van Rijn, a work which some have thought depicts the artist's sister, Liesbeth van Rijn; and the "Portrait of a Scholar" by Ferdinand Bol, one of Rembrandt's best pupils, are among the 17th-century works. Another of considerable human interest is the "Portrait of a Little Boy," painted by Ludolf de Jongh in 1661.

English painting is represented largely by portraits, although there is a fine landscape by John Constable, exhibited first at the Royal Academy in 1825. William Hogarth, George Romney, Thomas Gainsborough, Sir Joshua Reynolds, Sir Henry Raeburn and Sir Thomas Lawrence are prominent among the portraitists.

A well-documented painting of "Achilles on Sky-

99

ros'' (p. 90) by Nicolas Poussin (1594-1665) contains classical architectural details characteristic of this artist. Although a Frenchman, Poussin spent most of his life in Rome where he studiously turned to classical history and ancient mythology for his subject matter. By synthesizing this material into a heroic style of painting, his work became the prime example of 17th-century classicism and has been called, by some, the cornerstone of French painting.

"Battle on a Bridge" by Claude Lorrain, with its congested figures in a spacious vista of land and sea, and a small, 12 3/4-by-9 7/16-inch oil by Jean Antoine Watteau, "Le Lorgneur," one of several versions of the subject, join with the Poussin work to make a strong foundation for the French collection.

The typically active scene, "Amadis de Gaule Delivers a Damsel from Galpan's Castle," by Eugène Delacroix, provides a glimpse of French romanticism, while the Barbizon landscape school is well presented in paintings by Jean Baptiste Camille Corot, Diaz de la Peña, Jues Dupré and Théodore Rousseau.

A picture each by Claude Monet and Pierre Auguste Renoir introduce the modern period of French painting in which a still life by Georges Braque, heads by André Derain and Henri Matisse and a series of paintings by Picasso, from 1905 into the 1930's, are major pieces.

More than a dozen paintings by Jean Lurçat testify to T. Catesby Jones' interest in the artist. The collector's portrait head in bronze was executed by Jacques Lipchitz in 1941 and purchased by the museum.

Although the sculpture collection is small, it boasts a large bronze "Reclining Figure" of 1953-1954 by Henry Moore, a cubist-derived "Seated Man" in granite by Lipchitz and some earlier sculptures, including the small bronze "Theseus and the Centaur" by Antonio Canova.

An extensive collection of ancient Egyptian and classical Greek and Roman art and numerous examples of European decorative arts, tapestries, illuminations, stained glass, ceramics and silver round out the Virginia Museum collection. The most notable of the special collections, beyond a doubt, is the Pratt Col-

Below: Low Palace Relief. Assyria (885-869 B.C.). Alabaster. Firm conventions long dominated ancient art, the head being shown in profile, shoulders and arms from frontal view. *The Virginia Museum of Fine Arts*. Williams Fund purchase, 1956.

lection of Russian Imperial Jewels, numbering some 250 pieces by the Fabergé workshop, most of them executed for the Imperial family. Easter eggs of gold and silver, flowers and animals, usually of precious or semi-precious stones, make a very unusual display in an American museum.

One rather unusual but interesting decorative item is a 14th-century stained-glass window from the Church of St. Leonhard in Lavanttale, Austria (p. 89). An enchanting piece is the 4½-inches-long gold ''Puma'' (p.87), from Peru's Mochica Culture (c. 5th-11th centuries A.D.).

It seems entirely fitting that the fund left by Judge Payne, who gave the first pictures to the museum, should have been used to purchase Stuart Davis' ''Little Giant Still Life'' of 1950, the last picture in the 1961 catalogue of the Virginia Museum's 25th birthday celebration loan exhibition, ''Treasures in America.''

The Virginia Museum of Fine Arts: Richmond, Va. Open Tuesday through Saturday, 2 p.m. to 6 p.m., 8 p.m. to 10 p.m.; Sunday, 2 p.m. to 6 p.m. June 20 through Sept. 9, open Tuesday through Saturday, 11 a.m. to 5 p.m.; Sunday, 1 p.m. to 5 p.m. Closed national holidays.

Above: SCENE FROM THE GREEK WAR OF INDEPENDENCE by Théodore Géricault (1791-1924). Oil. *The Virginia Museum.*

Below: Imperial Easter Egg by Peter Carl Fabergé (19th century). Lapis lazuli, diamonds, gold. One of the Russian Imperial jewels by the workshop of Fabergé. *The Virginia Museum of Fine Arts.* Bequest of Lillian Thomas Pratt.

Below: LE LORGNEUR by Jean Antoine Watteau (1684-1721). Oil. A famous portrayal of aristocratic divertissements. *The Virginia Museum of Fine Arts.* Williams Fund Purchase, 1955.

IV MIDWEST

THE AKRON ART INSTITUTE

The Akron Art Institute was twice born in less than a quarter-century. Founded in 1920 to bring examples of the world's art to the people of Akron and for the education of their children in art, the institute was destroyed by fire in 1942.

Three years elapsed before it was possible to re-establish the museum in temporary quarters in the public library. Then funds were raised to remodel Akron's old Carnegie Library building for the purposes of the art institute, with its exhibitions and extensive educational programs for children and adults, including a professional art school, until this was discontinued in 1965. Informal art classes are maintained, however, and docents annually conduct thousands of school children through the museum.

With a small permanent collection, The Akron Art Institute relies on traveling exhibitions for many of its gallery shows, changing them as often as every month. From time to time, selections from the institute's holding are placed on view; there is a gallery set aside for showing the work of artists of the Akron region; and for many years a spring show has provided a review of the arts and crafts of the area.

While the works of art acquired by the museum are limited in number, there are some unusual pieces, and in very recent years notable additions have been made. In 1965 alone, one of four important purchases was the large panel painting of dramatic action with armed men and horses, "The Conversion of St. Paul," by the Flemish artist Hendrick de Clerck, whose life spanned the years 1570 to 1629.

Another 1965 purchase was the oval 17th-century Dutch "Portrait of a Burgher's Wife" by Nicolaes Eliasz.Picquenoy. The gentlewoman wearing lace and a great ruff collar, depicted in this work, contemplates the world with polite detachment. A French portrait and one by an American also entered the institute in that same year: Claude Lefebvre's "Portrait of a Magistrate" and the "Portrait of George Frederick Cooke, the Actor" painted by Thomas Sully.

Other Dutch and Flemish 17th-century paintings include "The Backgammon Players" by Dirck van Baburen; Frans Francken's "Tower of Babel," always a popular subject; a "Landscape" by Joos de Momper; and Peter Neefs' "Interior of Antwerp Cathedral at Night."

Chief among French paintings is "The Apotheosis of William the Silent" by Eugène Delacroix. The Italian holdings are headed by Alessandro Magnasco's "Woodcutter" and a "Madonna and Child" painted on a wood panel in egg tempera in the 15th or early 16th century.

Contemporary European art is represented through the work of the Belgian surrealist René Magritte, whose oil, "Les Pas Perdus," was painted in 1950. It depicts a mountainous scene with an enormous eagle jutting out of the nearest cliff as if carved from the solid rock, helping to enclose a mountain-ringed abyss with its immutable presence. Surrealism is a broad 20th-century movement, including a great range of styles, which has explored uncharted realms of the subconscious mind in the wake of Sigmund Freud's pioneering studies. Surrealist artists have turned fantasy and the irrational into major elements of 20th-century art, inviting the viewer to enter a dream world, as the Magritte work seems to do.

All of these paintings were acquired in the last dozen years, as were a number of American works. Landscapes by George Inness, Jasper Cropsey, Arthur H. Wyant and Childe Hassam; Morris Graves' "Hibernating Animal"; Milton Resnick's abstract expressionist canvas; and the bronze "Dolphin Fountain" by Gaston Lachaise all came by purchase or gift in this brief period.

A small collection of sculptured masks and figures from New Guinea, and a group of Chinese 19th-century rose quartz carvings, are recent gifts that add variety to the visitor's discoveries at The Akron Art Institute.

The Akron Art Institute: Akron, Ohio. Open Tuesday through Fri., 12 p.m. to 5 p.m.; Wednesday and Thursday evenings, 7 p.m. to 10 p.m.; Saturday, 9 a.m. to 5 p.m.; Sunday, 2 p.m. to 6 p.m. Closed Monday, national holidays and month of August.

Above: PORTRAIT OF A BURGHER'S WIFE by Nicolaes Eliasz. Picquenoy (1590-1653). Oil on copper. A gentlewoman of the mid-17th century, wearing a great white ruff collar, contemplates the world with polite detachment. *The Akron Art Institute.*

DES MOINES ART CENTER

One of the new museums of art that have sprung full-formed from the dreams of benefactors in the last quarter-century is the Des Moines Art Center, opened to the public in 1948 and housed in a world-renowned building designed for it by the great Finnish-American architect, Eliel Saarinen. The bequest of James D. Edmundson provided funds for the building and for museum operations, "as a gift to the city of Des Moines and to the people of his native state." A period of growth in facilities began in 1961 with the addition of school-wing galleries and a dining room. These were followed by a new sculpture court and auditorium wing.

The visitor to the art center will find sculpture by Carl Milles in the reflecting pool and fountain, as natural in association with Saarinen's architecture here as at Cranbrook in Bloomfield Hills, Michigan, where the two long were co-workers.

Indoors, finding a bronze by Henry Moore and sculpture by Henri Laurens, Jean Arp and Alexander Calder, with paintings by Joan Miró, Ben Nicholson, Oskar Kokoschka, Georges Rouault, Ernst Kirchner, Paul Klee and contemporary Americans, might suggest a purely modern orientation were it not for some works by Auguste Rodin, Jacob I. van Ruisdael, Francisco de Goya, Gustave Courbet, Camille Pissaro, Claude Monet and numerous 19th-century American painters.

Although late in the field, and almost of necessity required to specialize in 19th- and 20th-century art, the center has been fortunate in having funds and receiving gifts that make it possible to relate the present to the historic past by means of older works in the permanent collection as well as through temporary exhibitions.

A notable addition, announced in 1962, is the impressionist canvas, "Cliffs at Etretat," by Monet. This 26-by-32½-inch oil, dated 1886, is one of the series painted at Etretat on the English Channel, beginning in 1884. The high horizon allows but a small strip of clouded sky above the sea and the jutting cliff on the left, while below the waters dance and break among the remarkable craggy formations of rock.

Another artist inspired by wave-worn stones of the seashore, Henry Moore, recalled Monet's Etretat pictures of sea-sculptured rocks when discussing his own monumental bronze that stands in the reflecting pool at Lincoln Center in New York. The art center's "Seated Woman" by Moore, with its studio nickname "thin neck," to which one might add "small head," was purchased in 1964. Dated 1961, the five-foot-high erect, simplified figure, with its rugged surface, has elemental

Above: AMAZING JUGGLER by Yasuo Kuniyoshi (1893-1953). Oil. The artist's wistful message hints at the alienation of the entertainer. *Des Moines Art Center.* Edmundson Collection.

strength, as if reduced to something less than flesh yet more than bone.

The Monet was purchased with funds from the Nathan Emory Coffin Memorial which have also been used to acquire such paintings as Goya's portrait of "Don Manuel Garcia de la Prada"; the "Ville d'Avray" by Jean Baptiste Camille Corot, a small painting from the artist's most highly regarded period; the 1914 oil "Abstraction on Spectrum" by Stanton Macdonald-Wright, an important but often neglected American pioneer; and a watercolor by Kirchner. In recent years the Coffin Memorial has bought several outstanding sculptures, among them the work by Moore. Other recent acquisitions include the red clay ceramic "Matrimonial Couple," two seated figures of Mexican origin, dated between 100 B.C. and 500 A.D. and the subtly curved Cycladic idol figure (p. 107), a marble tomb

Above: AUNT FANNY by George Bellows (1882-1925). Oil. Bellows' portrait of his aunt was executed in 1920. His typical bravura in brushstroke is apparent and the great love he felt for the old woman is evident in the sensitively done hands and face. With patient amusement, she seems to wait for the painting to be finished. *Des Moines Art Center*. Edmundson Collection.

sculpture of the third millennium B.C. of particular interest to modern eyes because it is highly abstract in a geometric fashion.

The following year the Coffin Collection added the cubist-derived "Woman with Guitar," a complex system of planes composing a figure 15¾ inches high, carved in wood by the French sculptor Henri Laurens, and also the late, 1958, marble "Torse Gerbe" by Jean Arp, standing nearly four feet high. The suave rounded surfaces of the pure white stone allude to the graceful curves of the feminine figure while transcending specific representation of form.

Recent acquisitions such as the handsome Goya portrait; a 17th-century Dutch landscape by van Ruisdael; and "La Vallée de la Loue," a view of a rocky outcrop above still, reflecting water, by Courbet, suggests the energy with which the center has consistently been seeking historic depth for its collection.

Georges Rouault's "Vieux Faubourg" (p. 107) is another fine example of the scope of the collection. Rouault (1871-1958) is best known for paintings with intense colors heavily outlined in black and reminiscent of stained-glass work to which he was apprenticed as a youth, but the dominating qualities of his later painting, such as "Vieux Faubourg," are a subtle tenderness and a search for peace and harmony.

While European painting and sculpture provides some of the highlights of the Des Moines Art Center holdings, examples of American art are by no means lacking. With foresight and wisdom the center has acquired works by important artists still comparatively unrecognized, such as Macdonald-Wright and Jerome Myers, as well as established Americans, including John Sloan, George Bellows and Edward Hopper, whose paintings are becoming progressively harder to collect as they enter public museums across the nation.

Myers' pastel, "Sunday in the Park," is the work of an artist instrumental in organizing the 1913 Amory

(Continued on page 111)

Below: CLIFFS AT ETRETAT by Claude Monet (1840-1926). Oil. Broad and restless brushstrokes result in a decisive interpretation done by Monet in 1886 at Etretat on the English Channel. *Des Moines Art Center.* Nathan Emory Coffin Memorial Collection.

Midwestern Museums

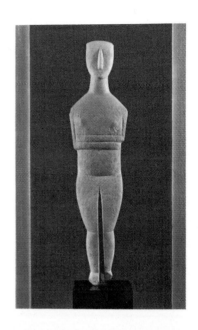

Right: Cycladic Idol Figure. Marble. (Third millennium B.C.) The ancient Cycladic culture was located on the Aegean Sea, and is noted largely for its subtly curved, highly abstracted idols. *Des Moines Art Center.* The Nathan Emory Coffin Memorial Collection.

Below: VIEUX FAUBOURG by Georges Rouault (1871-1958). Oil. The elements of desolation and tenderness in Rouault's work come from his disturbing memories of Paris' working class suburbs. *Des Moines Art Center.* The Nathan Emory Coffin Memorial Collection.

Above: SEAL ROCKS by Ralph Blakelock (1846-1919). Oil. Reverence for the primeval wilderness influenced all Blakelock's deeply glowing works. Scorned by critics, he was forced to sell his paintings for small sums. Poverty and despair drove him to insanity before his genius was recognized and rewarded shortly before his death. *The Paine Art Center and Arboretum.*

Left: TWO GIRLS AT THE PIANO by Pierre Renoir (1841-1919). Oil. Never a theorist, Renoir found and captured on canvas the graciousness and charm of the women he took such delight in painting. *Joslyn Art Museum.*

Below: AUTOMAT by Edward Hopper (1882-1967). Oil. Part of Hopper's greatness is the ability to bring a passionate significance to lonely and unguarded moments, and to find nobility in ordinary people and their everyday life. *Des Moines Art Center.* Edmundson Collection.

Above: MAN WITH A FALCON by Titian (Tiziano Vecelli) (1477-1576). Oil. European rulers competed for the honor of owning portraits and poetical compositions by this master of the Venetian School and Italian Renaissance, whose dominant hallmarks are the use of rich color and a profound concern for the nuances of light. *Joslyn Museum of Art.*

Above: A WOODY SCENE NEAR THE HAGUE by Jacob I. van Ruisdael (1630-1681). Oil. Little noted during his life, the Dutch artist is now acclaimed for his poetic landscapes. *Des Moines Art Center*. Nathan Emory Coffin Memorial Collection.

(Continued from page 106)

Show that rudely awakened American art lovers from their pleasant reveries amid 19th-century academic pieces. Myers' painting is related to that of Maurice Prendergast who exhibited with "The Eight"; three more of that group, Robert Henri, Ernest Lawson and Sloan, are represented in the art center.

Another American artist of repute who is represented in the Des Moines collection is Hopper (1882-1967). Hopper was a student of Henri at the New York School of Art, where he studied from 1900 to 1906. But his work did not follow that of Henri and "The Eight." In fact, Hopper never became part of any particular school, but, usually impervious to outside influences, he developed his own unique style, marked by a feeling for repose, the silence of open spaces and the picturesque aspects of commonplace scenes. "Automat" (p. 109) at Des Moines is representative of his work in several ways: The subject is American and ordinary, the open space of the composition emphasizes the loneliness and quiet of the night, and the people depicted are wrapped in their individual worlds.

Bellows' 1920 portrait, "Aunt Fanny" is one of his penetrating studies, executed with typical bravura in brushwork but with great sensitivity in the expressive face and hands of the elderly woman. Arthur Dove, John Marin, Mary Cassatt, Charles Burchfield, Lyonel Feininger, George O. Hart, John Singer Sargent, Max Weber, Milton Avery and Yasuo Kuniyoshi are other Americans in the "hard-to-find" class whose works are in the collection.

American landscapists include George Inness, Henry Ward Ranger, Willard Metcalf and Childe Hassam. Ralph A. Blakelock's "Fifty-Ninth Street in 1864" is a very small oil, as is the one by Inness. Executed in an unusual medium, the oil monotypes by Lawson, Sloan and Hart are unique prints, offset from paintings in oil on glass or another non-absorbent surface.

Contemporary American works are growing in number through gifts and purchases. Sue Fuller's "String Composition No. 105," an abstract pattern of saran threads, and Harry Bertoia's bronze "Dandelion" are recently acquired sculptures. A cross section of styles is provided by the paintings of Henry Varnum Poor, Kyle Morris, Jack Levine, John Koch, Byron Burford and Raymond Parker.

Collections of Oriental and African art have been started, but the most spectacular recent addition is the Rosenfield Graphic Art Collection, for which more than 30 prints were acquired in 1963-1964 alone, ranging from the 15th through the 20th centuries.

The aspiration behind the Des Moines Art Center's ambitious development may very well be expressed in the Milles fountain group "Pegasus and Bellerophon," for, after capturing the winged horse, Bellerophon conquered all enemies and finally attempted to rise to the heavens.

Des Moines Art Center: Des Moines, Iowa. Open Tuesday through Saturday, 11 a.m. to 5 p.m.; Thursday, 11 a.m. to 9 p.m.; Sunday and holidays, 1 p.m. to 6 p.m. Closed Monday.

GALLERIES OF CRANBROOK ACADEMY OF ART

Influential out of proportion to its size because its graduates have been able and its faculty excellent, the Cranbrook Academy of Art is set in landscaped grounds accented by the sculpture and fountain groups of Carl Milles, who for 21 years was a sculptor in residence. The Galleries of Cranbrook Academy of Art occupy a trim modern building, still fresh in style after more than 25 years, that was designed by the great Finnish architect Eliel Saarinen, who was the first president of the academy.

Cranbrook's beginnings go back to 1927, when the publisher George C. Booth and his wife Ellen Scripps Booth brought together informally a group of artists and craftsmen and established the Cranbrook Foundation. The idea of an association of practicing artists and advanced students attained realization with the formation of the Academy of Art, accredited by the National Association of Schools of Art, chartered in 1942 as an institution of higher learning by the State of Michigan and accredited by the North Central Association of Colleges and Secondary Schools in 1960.

The Booths' gifts, in time, established six independently governed institutions on their 300-acre estate in Bloomfield Hills, Michigan, ten miles north of the Detroit city limits. In addition to the Academy of Art, there are the Brookside School for coeducational elementary education; the Cranbrook School and Kingswood School for secondary schooling of boys and girls respectively; Christ Church with artistic treasures from the 12th century to the present; and the Gardens of Cranbrook House.

The Cranbrook School, completed in 1927, is prize-winning architecture, the first major work designed by Eliel Saarinen after coming to the United States. In 1941 his Cranbrook Academy of Art Galleries building at last provided adequate housing for the permanent collection, temporary exhibitions and student exhibits.

Because Cranbrook is primarily a school of art, the principal role of the art galleries is to keep the community of artists and art students abreast with contemporary work and to show relevant historical materials. Accordingly, the permanent collection of contemporary, Oriental and pre-Columbian art frequently gives way to the special loan exhibitions that constitute the major activity of the galleries.

Prominent among the works in the permanent collection is the large "Reclining Figure," carved in wood

Above: The circular "Orpheus Fountain" with its slim bronze youths and maidens typifies the many sculptures created by Carl Milles (1875-1955) to be found at Cranbrook Academy.

Above: (left) HEAD OF BODHISATTVA. China, T'ang Dynasty (618-907 A.D.). Wood. During the reigns of the 20 sovereigns who ruled in the T'ang period, the Chinese Empire reached the height of its power and the zenith of cultural development, notably in poetry, painting and sculpture. Center: RECLINING FIGURE by Henry Moore (1898-   ). Wood. One of Moore's huge reclining figures stressing both solidity and void in his concept of mass. *Galleries of Cranbrook Academy of Art.*

by Henry Moore. Oriental and pre-Columbian pieces, as well as a variety of paintings and sculptures, came to the Cranbrook Galleries through benefactions of the founder, Mr. Booth.

The buildings and grounds of Cranbrook are rich in sculpture by Carl Milles (1875-1955), for pieces large and small are to be found in many places. On either side of the great pillared porch of the art galleries is a noble fountain. The circular "Orpheus Fountain," with its ring of slim bronze youths and maidens around a central mist of water, is on the north side, and contrasts with the reflecting pool of the "Triton Fountain" on the south. At the head of the pool stands the great "Europa and the Bull," while not far away to the north, beside another body of water, a bronze "Jonah and the Whale" overlook Jonah Pool.

Like Saarinen, Milles was a great creative influence at Cranbrook. Born Carl Emil Wilhelm Anderson at Lagga in Upsala, Sweden, the sculptor was schooled in Stockholm and Paris. After building a reputation through heroic-sized monuments for cities in his native land, Milles moved to the United States in 1929, and in 1931 joined the staff at Cranbrook where he made his home and studio until he returned to Sweden shortly before his death.

Galleries of Cranbrook Academy of Art: Bloomfield Hills, Michigan. Open Tuesday through Sunday, 1 p.m. to 5 p.m.

HERRON MUSEUM OF ART

Every section of the country has been affected by the invigorating cultural contagion that is stirring old organizations and inspiring new ones. The Art Association of Indianapolis, incorporated in 1883, which governs the Herron School of Art and the Herron Museum of Art, was aroused by prospects and plans for a tremendous expansion by the gift in 1966 of a 42-acre estate and its 22-room mansion from the family of the late Mr. and Mrs. J. K. Lilly, Jr.

The beautifully landscaped grounds, made into public gardens and a park, and the 18th-century French styled residence, used to exhibit decorative arts, will be maintained as a memorial to the Lillys. On the grounds, the art association's new museum and auditorium promise to give Indianapolis a major cultural center.

Meanwhile, the extensive and rapidly growing collections of painting, sculpture and the decorative arts are crowding the building that has served since it was erected in 1906, following the bequest of John Herron. Since 1884, in addition to exhibitions, the association has endeavored to provide instruction in art. A school was started and a building erected in 1929, and in 1962 a new structure gave the Herron School of Art much improved facilities.

While the Herron Museum collections include examples of African, pre-Columbian, Near Eastern, Far Eastern, Greek and Roman art, the major holdings are of European and American painting from various periods, with some sculpture.

As with others of the older regional museums, the collection at first simply accumulated by gifts and occasional purchases, without any particular direction. By this method some excellent works entered the museum on their face value rather than through fashion or to fulfill a plan.

The John Herron Fund bought oils by Childe Hassam and Frank Duvenek in 1901 and by William Merritt Chase in 1889 and 1903 when they were popular, and the museum has acquired works by the last two as

Below: PORT OF GRAVELINES, PETIT FORT PHILIPPE by Georges Seurat (1859-1891). Oil. Effects of diffused light and atmosphere are produced through juxtaposing tiny dots of the primary colors in systematic patterns. *Herron Museum of Art.*

recently as 1957-1958, when they are on the verge of becoming fashionable. Two paintings by Arthur B. Davies came by purchase and gift in 1930 and 1931, a watercolor by Charles Burchfield in 1931, and an oil by Edward Hopper, also in 1931, long before their vogue. A pastel by Mary Cassatt, "Two Young Girls," was bought in 1925, a year before her death.

Yet by far the largest acquisition of major works, both English and American, has taken place in the last three decades, to enlarge the collection and to fill gaps. Among them are pictures by Jean Auguste Dominique Ingres, François Boucher, Jean Baptiste Siméon Chardin, Gustave Courbet, Claude Monet, Pierre Auguste Renoir, Georges Seurat, Paul Cézanne, Pablo Picasso, Henri Matisse and Georges Braque; by Rembrandt van Rijn, Sir Anthony van Dyke, Meindert Hobbema, Pieter Claesz, Aelbert Cuyp, David Teniers the Younger, Gerard ter Borch and Jacob I. van Ruisdael; by Francesco Bassano, Taddeo Gaddi, Francesco Guardi and Antonio Canaletto; by the great English portrait and landscape painters; and by leading Americans from Gilbert Stuart through the Hudson River School, "The Eight," to Hans Hofmann and Andrew Wyeth.

"Port of Gravelines, Petit Fort Philippe" by Seurat (1859-1891), painted in 1890, is one of the last works of the pointillist who died so young. Pointillism or "divisionism," as it is also called, was a method of painting Seurat developed which was based on scientific color theories regarding the nature of light and the vision of color. Seurat's method, in which he was followed for a time by Paul Signac and Camille Pissarro, gained vibrant visual effects by breaking color tones into minute touches of their component hues, thus pointillism or divisionism. In the Herron work, Seurat used this style as a means of expressing, as few artists have succeeded in doing, the atmosphere of the sea in a moment of calm, with boats beached or riding at anchor, the long horizon interrupted by vertical masts and a lighthouse tower, while the great curving sweep of the quay and a few angled spars alone break the stillness of vertical reflections.

Chief among the seven works by J.M.W. Turner, two of them watercolors bought in 1913, is "The Fifth Plague of Egypt," a four-by-six-foot canvas with a sweeping circular composition centered on a pyramid.

From the two large Spanish Romanesque frescoes portraying "The Marriage at Cana" and "Christ's Entry into Jerusalem" and dated about 1200, to the avant-garde paintings of the last few years, the Herron Museum of Art has much to offer under the direction of new imaginative leadership. In addition to its permanent collections, the visitor will find one or more special exhibitions on view.

Above: THE TRIUMPH OF THE DOMINICAN ORDER by Francesco Solimena (1657-1747). The great decorative phase of Neopolitan art rose to international importance with the work of Solimena and his followers. *Herron Museum of Art.*

Herron Museum of Art: Indianapolis, Ind. Open Tuesday through Saturday, 10 a.m. to 5 p.m.; Sunday, 1 p.m. to 6 p.m. Closed July 4, Thanksgiving and Christmas.

JOSLYN ART MUSEUM

Not content with mere acquisition of American and European art to educate the public, the Joslyn Art Museum, in Omaha, Nebraska, makes a special and unique effort to interpret and explain the fine arts in relation to the historical and utilitarian background of each period.

Inside the imposing marble structure built in 1928-1931, which must be increased in size by one-third to meet present and expected needs, the spacious main floor holds the Floral Court, containing Oriental art, and the large concert hall which together form an east-west center flanked by exhibition galleries. The five south galleries lead the visitor from the ancient world through the 19th century, while five north galleries display contemporary arts from the permanent collections and temporary exhibitions.

Galleries devoted to the permanent collections offer a rich diet of visual experience in painting, sculpture and decorative arts, set in historical context by means of special photographic and dioramic display cases. For example, a photograph of the Parthenon forms the background for Greek statuary and vases in the gallery devoted to the classical world. Again, nearby the museum's famed Venetian masterpiece, Titian's "Man with a Falcon" (p. 110), is a display case with small sculpture and a view of the Doges' Palace in Venice for background.

Titian (born Tiziano Vecelli) (c. 1477-1576), once a student of Giovanni Bellini, is considered the foremost painter of the Venetian School. While Titian was receiving his training there, Venice was a wealthy, cosmopolitan city. It seemed ripe for conquest by an artist of Titian's great talent and after about 1518 he began to receive many offers of commissions from dukes, kings and princes of the Church. He was especially successful as a portraitist because he was able to depict each sitter with great sympathy. This quality, which his contemporaries called "the poetry of Titian," is apparent in "Man with a Falcon," which was painted about 1530. That was the year he met Holy Roman Emperor Charles V, who became his patron and for whom Titian painted the greater part of his works for half a century.

The permanent "Life on the Prairie" exhibition illustrates with works of art, many artifacts and photographs the history of 10,000 years in Nebraska, from the aboriginal past, through exploration and settlement, to the present day. Completely furnished period rooms are included, while artist-explorers of the 18th and 19th centuries are represented by paintings and prints.

Works by George Catlin, Karl Bodmer, Alfred Jacob Miller and many others of the artists who accompanied expeditions, or simply set out to make a pictorial record of the new lands and their peoples, have been included, and the paintings by several of the Hudson River School, Albert Beirstadt, Thomas Moran and T. Worthington Whittredge among them, broaden the scope of the exhibit. Displays by contemporary painters and designer-craftsmen complete the story.

The Joslyn Art Museum stands as a monument to the Vermonters, George A. Joslyn and his wife Sarah, who came to Omaha in 1879 and made a great fortune. After her husband's death in 1916, Mrs. Joslyn devoted 12 years to planning a memorial to perpetuate the Joslyns' interest in art and music in a cultural center for the benefit of all citizens. The museum building, which was valued at $3,000,000 when it opened in 1931, has grown to become a $20,000,000 fine arts facility. In 1966 plans were announced for a $3,000,000 wing.

Mrs. Joslyn established the Society of Liberal Arts (now the Joslyn Liberal Arts Society) to own and operate the museum, giving an endowment to assure its maintenance. It remains as a private institution, dedicated to public service, and is one of the few fine

Above: PORTRAIT OF THE MARQUESA DE FONTANA by Francisco de Goya (1746-1828). Oil. Goya took recognition of subject's womanliness. *Joslyn Art Museum,* Omaha, Nebraska.

Above: BUFFALO HERDS ON THE UPPER MISSOURI by Karl Bodmer (1809-1893). Oil. The collection from which this painting comes represents Joslyn's unique effort to interpret the arts in relation to the historical background of America, and includes 427 sketches from Bodmer's Missouri expedition. *Joslyn Art Museum*, Omaha, Nebraska. Northern Natural Gas Company Collection.

arts centers in the nation still without tax support. Gifts of private art collections aided the museum's growth in early years, and at the time of her death in 1940, Mrs. Joslyn bequeathed the bulk of her estate to the society, thus making funds available for some major art purchases.

The year 1942 was a great one for the Joslyn Art Museum because so many paintings bearing the names of famous artists entered the collection. Together with the Titian, there was Rembrandt van Rijn's "Dirk van Os," Lorenzo di Credi's "Madonna and Child and Two Angels," Veronese's "Venus at Her Toilette," Francisco de Goya's "Portrait of the Marquesa de Fontana," El Greco's "St. Francis in Prayer," Sir Anthony van Dyck's "Portrait of a Flemish Lady" and Jean Baptiste Camille Corot's "River Scene, Chateau-Thierry."

In 1944, Pierre Auguste Renoir's "Two Young Girls at the Piano" (p. 109) was bought as a good example of one of the artist's favorite subjects. A rare, nearly life-size portrait sculpture in granite of Queen Amenirdas I of Egypt's 25th Dynasty was purchased in 1953. It is one of three portraits of her in the round known to exist; the others are in Cairo and Sydney.

"St. Jerome" by Jusepe de Ribera; the polychrome 15th-century Italian terra-cotta "St. Petronius"; the bronze "Eve" by Auguste Rodin; a 12th-century Byzantine stone relief from near Venice; and "St. Paul the Apostle," a 13th-century Sienese marble sculpture

Above: SAINT FRANCIS IN PRAYER by El Greco (Domenicos Theotocopoulos) (1541-1614). Oil. A mystical and ethereal depiction of the saint. *Joslyn Art Museum*, Omaha, Nebraska.

thought to be from the workshop of Giovanni Pisano, were among the most acclaimed additions to the Joslyn Collection in recent years.

While these classics attract attention, the museum has not neglected American art of the 19th and 20th centuries. One of the most modern examples — modern in nature and conception, rather than in newness, since it has been around for several decades — is Thomas Wilfred's "Lumia — Space-Time Study, Opus 135," a development from Wilfred's invention, the Clavilux. In a darkened room, on a small screen that easily becomes a window looking out into a vast cosmos, Lumia plays moving lights that shift in color and form in seemingly endless variations. Few museums can offer this experience, which is infinitely more satisfying than the flashing lights and vigorous action of the usual kinetic light arts of today.

The 19th-century and early 20th-century Americans are highlighted by works of George Inness, Winslow Homer, William M. Harnett, Mary Cassatt, John Marin and most of "The Eight." Grant Wood's landscape of hard-edged fields and trees, and Thomas Hart Benton's dramatic "Hailstorm," a scene of farmers plowing caught in a sudden blast, with forked lightning from a stormy sky, add a regional touch, as does Frederic Remington's "Bronco Buster," a bronze cast.

Modern sculpture includes the spirited "Laughing Girl," a bust, by Sir Jacob Epstein, and Jacques Lipchitz's "Hagar."

Perhaps the greatest single collection, displayed on the balcony level and in the Maximilian-Bodmer Room on the ground floor, is the Maximilian-Bodmer Collection of 427 original sketches by Karl Bodmer,

the young Swiss artist who accompanied Prince Alexander Philip Maximilian on the expedition to the upper Missouri River in 1833-1834. In addition to pictures, there are numerous original documents, some unpublished, the metal engraving plates from which the color-prints were made for Prince Maximilian's book, *Travels in the Interior of North America,* and many other objects relating to the expedition.

This remarkable treasure, carefully stored in the archives of Neuwied Castle where Maximilian was born, was "lost" for nearly 100 years until rediscovered in 1950. Purchased and owned by the Northern Natural Gas Company of Omaha, the collection is housed in the Joslyn Art Museum, which is its custodian.

By a similar arrangement the 109 watercolor sketches made in the field by Alfred Jacob Miller on an expedition to the Wind River Mountains of Wyoming in 1837 are on display. They also are lent by the Northern Natural Gas Company. An outstanding collection of Indian art of North America and collections of portrait and documentary photographs enrich the unparalleled opportunities for study of the American West available at the museum.

With long-range plans for expansion that include a Historical Wing with a Regional Prairie Museum and a Science-Space Wing with a planetarium, all in association with art and music, the activities of the Joslyn Liberal Arts Society continue to fulfill the intentions of the founders to integrate the fine arts with the creative practical arts.

Joslyn Art Museum: Omaha, Neb. Open Tuesday through Saturday, 10 a.m. to 5 p.m.; Thursday, 10 a.m. to 9 p.m.; Sunday, 1 p.m. to 5 p.m. Closed Monday and holidays.

Below: BRONCO BUSTER by Frederic Remington (1861-1909). Bronze. In vigorous sculpture and painting the artist recorded the West which still lives in the minds of many. *Joslyn Art Museum*, Omaha, Nebraska. Bequest of N. P. Dodge.

Above: SAINT JEROME by Jusepe de Ribera (1591-1652). Oil. The religious art of the Counter Reformation aimed at convincing the beholder of its truth by avoiding the mystical and emulating the reality of the event. Ribera was a master at imparting this sense of the immediate, the tactile and the actual in his Spanish Baroque style. *Joslyn Art Museum,* Omaha, Nebraska.

THE PAINE ART CENTER AND ARBORETUM

In the luxurious setting of an English-styled country house, intentionally incorporating architectural features from the 15th through the 19th centuries, the Paine Art Center, Oshkosh, Wisconsin, presents its collection of English silver, Islamic carpets of the late 17th through the 19th century and other decorative arts. A large picture gallery holds many of the 19th-century pictures, while the rest of the collection is distributed through rooms appropriately furnished according to the styles and tastes of 300 years.

Although the mansion was built in the late 1920's, it was not completed until after founder Nathan Paine's death in 1947. A year later when interior furnishings were complete, it opened to the public as a privately supported contribution to the cultural life of the community in which the Paine Lumber Company had flourished for three generations.

The painting collection primarily reflects a taste for landscape and genre, with a scattering of portraits and some still-life subjects. Most of the pictures are relatively small, except for the salon paintings, of which "Morning on the Oise" by Charles-François Daubigny (1817-1878) is a major example.

Daubigny is linked with Jean Baptiste Camille Corot, also represented in the collection by a small painting. Both were leading artists associated with the Barbizon School of landscapists that flourished near Fountainebleau in the second half of the 19th century. Others of the Barbizon group whose works are in the art center are Jules Dupré, Diaz de la Peña, Charles Emile Jacque, Théodore Rousseau and Jean François Millet.

"Morning on the Oise," which was first shown in the Paris Salon of 1866, the year it was painted, was purchased by Nathan Paine in 1927. A fresh pastoral scene of green meadows, wooded hills and calm water, it derives scale from a few small figures on the banks of the river and in the fields. In 1904 it was exhibited in St. Louis at the Louisiana Purchase Exposition, and in 1964, at the Huntington Hartford Gallery of Modern

Below: MORNING ON THE OISE by Charles-François Daubigny (1817-1878). Oil. First exhibited at the Paris Salon of 1886, this pastoral scene of green meadows and calm waters derives its scale from a few small figures standing on the banks and in the fields. The work was purchased by Nathan Paine for his collection in 1927. *The Paine Art Center and Arboretum.*

Above: OFF THE COAST OF CORNWALL by George Inness (1825-1894). Oil. Inness' later works were concerned less with detail, about which he had been meticulous in earlier years. His technique became simpler, and his primary motivation was to capture the elemental, emotional and transitory facets in the landscapes he painted. *The Paine Art Center and Arboretum.*

Art in New York. In May of 1964 the Paine Art Center presented the first American retrospective exhibition of paintings, drawings and prints by Daubigny, borrowing from many museums and private collections, in which the art center's picture was a center piece.

English portraiture is represented by Joseph Wright's likenesses of a woman and a gentleman, unidentified, painted in the second half of the 18th century. Also in the Georgian Room is one of the many portraits of George Washington of the Athenaeum type, which was declared by C. M. Mount, author of a definitive biography of Gilbert Stuart, to be definitely by the painter's own hand rather than by his daughter, Jane Stuart, to whom it previously had been tentatively ascribed.

American landscape painting in the Paine Art Center includes work by artists whose names are associated with the Hudson River School — George Inness, Alexander H. Wyant, Thomas Moran, Homer Martin and Ralph A. Blakelock — but they worked in the style only briefly in their early years.

Blakelock (1846-1919) — whose "Seal Rocks" (p. 108), painted around 1880, is a fine example of his moody, partly impressionistic and luminous style — set out ambitiously at the age of 22 to paint the American West. The highly emotional artist traveled across the plains and Rockies to California, everywhere sketching the landscape and Indians and developing a fascination for the wilderness which forever influenced his art.

121

However, with his large family to support, he was finally subdued by the struggle of making a living with his art. On the day his ninth child was born, he was offered $500 for a painting he was trying to sell for twice that. At first refusing the counteroffer, later the same day he returned to accept it, but was then offered only $300. Blakelock frantically tore up the money and was taken into custody and found insane. By 1916, before he died in an asylum, his paintings sold for as much as $20,000.

Inness (1825-1894), whose European experience brought him into contact with Barbizon painters, cleared the path for some of these Americans who followed him into a softer, more atmospheric treatment of landscape. Among the three paintings by Inness, the one of particular interest is "Off the Coast of Cornwall, England," a seascape painted in 1887, a rare subject for the artist. It is assumed to have been based on studies made when he visited England in 1870, and shows small boats caught in the breaking surf.

Two especially interesting American pieces are bronze sculptures by Frederic Remington — "The Rattle-snake," done in 1905, and "The Bronco Buster," first cast in 1895. These works formed the basis for the important 1967 exhibition of 75 works by Remington in various media, and later shown at the Minneapolis Institute of Arts.

Thomas Moran, born in England in 1837 and brought to America at the age of seven, painted his small "Yellowstone Canyon" in 1919 at the age of 82. Earlier he had traveled in the American West to gather material for large panoramas of the dramatic landscape, from which this 20-by-16-inch canvas derives.

Later Americans include Winslow Homer, whose watercolor, "Lake St. John, Canada," was painted in 1895, and early 20th-century artists D. W. Tryon, J. F. Murphy and John Costigan. Although other 20th-century paintings are on the walls, Nathan Paine's taste remained consistent with the manorial setting so that the harmony of the art center was not disturbed.

The Paine Art Center and Arboretum: Oshkosh, Wis. Open Sun., Tuesday, Thursday and Saturday, 2 p.m. to 5 p.m.; daily (Memorial Day to Labor Day), 2 p.m. to 5 p.m. Closed Monday and holidays.

Above: The elegant Georgian dining room in The Paine Art Center and Arboretum displays fine 18th-century furnishings.

P. Richard Eells

Above: THE RATTLESNAKE by Frederic Remington (1861-1909). Bronze, cast, 1905. *Paine Art Center and Arboretum.*

Above: GEORGE WASHINGTON by Gilbert Stuart (1755-1828). Oil. Stuart painted General Washington three times. This likeness, hanging in the Georgian dining room, had previously been attributed to the artist's daughter. *The Paine Art Center and Arboretum.*

THE UNIVERSITY OF KANSAS MUSEUM OF ART

There is more to running an art museum than just collecting the objects and arranging them for display on gallery walls and sculpture stands. The important things are not so obvious to the museum visitor: knowing what to collect, where to search for it, and authenticating the objects secured by scientific examination and by unearthing their histories.

One of the major challenges facing any museum director or curator is to look hard at a presumed treasure, whether offered as a gift or for sale, to learn what it really is, whether or not there is a glamorous name and voluminous provenance attached.

Where better than at a university can this task of study and verification be accomplished? Under the direction of distinguished art historians, the careful preparation and display of paintings, sculpture, prints and drawings, together with publication of scholarly articles on the collection in the *Register* of the museum, make The University of Kansas Museum of Art outstanding among regional art institutions, while the scope and variety of its holdings make it as interesting as it is instructive.

Primarily concerned with the paintings and sculpture of the Western world from ancient times to the present, this museum of art from its inception has served the university and its community as an educational enterprise. Beginning with the William Bridges Thayer Memorial Collection in 1917, it was augmented in the late 1950's by the Samuel H. Kress Study Collection, and in every year it has been sustained and expanded by many individual gifts.

Only a few of the major works can be described, starting with the remarkable lindenwood "Madonna and Child," carved by Tilman Riemenschneider (c. 1462-1531) about 1499, which came to the museum in 1951 from the collection of the Prince of Liechtenstein, whose vaults in 1967 yielded the National Gallery of Art's "Ginevra de' Benci" by Leonardo da Vinci.

Standing nearly four feet high, the lovely figure with serene countenance was given an active pose, as if in motion, enhanced by the angular sweep and flow of drapery and intensified by the twisting figure of the Child who turns back to the Madonna with an awkward, vigorous thrust of His arms. The sculpture is acknowledged to be one of the finest by Riemenschneider in the United States.

Another and quite different carving is the Baroque ivory "Judith and Holofernes," which is only eight inches high. Judith stands astride the hunched up figure

Above: MADONNA AND CHILD by Tilman Riemenschneider (1462-1531). Lindenwood. Madonna in active pose conveys the illusion of motion. *University of Kansas Museum of Art.*

of the dead Holofernes, holding his head in her left hand and a short, heavy sword in her right. She is broad shouldered and muscular, nude except for a garment that enfolds her waist. On her face is an expression of horror rather than triumph, and she looks beyond rather than at the dreadful trophy she holds.

Although the letters "B" and "G" appear on the sword blade, the sculptor's identity is shrouded, known only through other works, mainly reliefs, bearing similar initials and dated in the second half of the 17th century.

Two life-size 18th-century figures in painted and gilded lindenwood now are identified as "St. Damian" and "St. Cosmas," patron saints of trades and professions concerned with healing. As twins, they are similar in appearance and dress. Their florid gestures and sweeping robes are further agitated by broken surfaces cut to create a play of light over the white painted drapery with gilded edging. Attributed to Joseph Götsch, they may have formed part of the richly ornamented interior of some Rococo church in Bavaria.

Among many other excellent sculptures in wood and bronze are four Apostles, between 17 and 18 inches high and carved in wood, that are tentatively placed as French works of the 15th century. Detailed, expressive faces, veined hands and clearly differentiated treatment of the robes, suggest a carefully composed grouping for an altarpiece.

Turning from sculpture to painting, the Kress Collection gave the museum some of its earliest pieces. Among them is the tiny seven-by-nine-inch 14th-century panel painting attributed to Guiduccio Palmerucci. It depicts the "Madonna and Child between Two Angels, with a Kneeling Donor, His Wife and Child," the latter appearing as small suppliant figures in the lower foreground. Another interesting work is the colorful 15th-century "Madonna and Child" by Cenni di Francesco, in which the happy Child holds a bird by one wing in His left hand while His right is raised in blessing. An ornate floral background offsets the gilded ground and complements the Madonna's red gown.

An appealing work of the late Renaissance, attributed to the 16th-century Florentine painter, Agnolo Bronzino, is the shoulder-length portrait of a "Florentine Lady as the Magdalene." Holding the white alabaster ointment jar that is St. Mary Magdalene's attribute, the beautiful young woman wears a scarf of yellow and pink over a warm green tunic, painted with Bronzino's clarity and precision.

Other notable portraits include the 17th-century matching pair by the Netherlander Nicolas Maes, of a lady and a gentleman, and the striking depiction of "Baptist May, Esq." by Gerald Soest, who worked in England during the 17th century.

Bronze portrait heads of Albert Einstein and T. S.

Above: ST. COSMAS by Joseph Götsch. Painted and gilded lindenwood. A patron saint of the professions and trades concerned with healing. *The University of Kansas Museum of Art.*

Eliot by Sir Jacob Epstein and one of Renoir by Aristide Maillol, are strong representations of modern European art. American works include a grisaille oil sketch dated 1782, "The Inspiration of the Prophet Isaiah," by Benjamin West, one of his studies for ambitious decorations of a chapel in Windsor Castle commissioned by George III but abandoned after the King became insane

Above: FAUST IN HIS STUDY by Rembrandt Van Rijn (1606-1669). Etching. It is doubtful that the artist drew Faust specifically. The designation possibly came from a Parisian who apparently used some of his engravings for philosophers' portraits. More probably an alchemist is pictured conjuring a spirit which appears as a radiant circle, the enclosed letters forming an anagram indicating the limits of human knowledge. *The University of Kansas Museum.* Gift of Senator August Lauterbach.

Above: BALLAD OF THE JEALOUS LOVER OF LONE GREEN VALLEY by Thomas Hart Benton (1889-   ). Oil on masonite panel. Gift of The Elizabeth M. Watkins Fund of the Endowment Association. *The University of Kansas Museum of Art.*

in 1810; and also Rembrandt Peale's 1812 portrait of "Mrs. John Brice and Child."

Later American pictures include works by several members of the Hudson River School, two watercolors by Winslow Homer, an oil by George Inness and several works by members of "The Eight." Appropriately for a Kansas museum, paintings by Kansan John Steuart Curry and Missourian Thomas Hart Benton are also in the collection. Among the 19th- and 20th-century European works in the collection are paintings by Edouard Manet, Claude Monet, Maillol and Otto Dix. Such contemporary works indicate that the museum includes art of the present in its educational program, which also is carried on through six or more temporary exhibitions every year.

The small Far Eastern collection contains some excellent pieces and is earmarked for expansion. The growing collection of graphic arts includes prints by early masters like Martin Schongauer and Albrecht Dürer, as well as modern prints by Henri de Toulouse-Lautrec, Mary Cassatt, Henry Matisse, Pablo Picasso and others.

The University of Kansas Museum of Art was founded when Sallie Casey Thayer donated her collection in 1917. In 1924 the Thayer Collection was installed in Spooner Hall, a heavy stone structure designed as a library. The remodeled building served until the end of the 1940's when it was modernized to accommodate the growing collections under the direction of John Maxon. A few years later Edward A. Maser rehung the museum when the Kress Study Collection arrived.

Through its scholarly tradition, the museum has set standards of excellence in the presentation and interpretation of the fine arts, and the success of its program of education is seen in the continued growth in the number and quality of its holdings.

The University of Kansas Museum of Art: Lawrence, Kans. Open Mon. through Saturday, 9 a.m. to 4:45 p.m.; Sunday, 1:30 p.m. to 4:45 p.m. Closed Thanksgiving, Christmas, New Year's and Independence Day.

WALKER ART CENTER

The Walker Art Center in Minneapolis is one of America's oldest art centers. Especially famous today for initiating contemporary exhibitions, the Walker is a descendant of the first art gallery in the Midwest that was open to the public. Built in 1879, that original gallery was a skylighted room, attached to Thomas Barlow Walker's home, 16-by-30 feet in size, and was furnished with an exhibition of 20 paintings. Three more rooms were added in 1892 for the display of the expanding collection, which extended from paintings and prints to bronzes, miniatures and examples of Greek and Roman art and artifacts.

T. B. Walker was engaged in building a lumber empire when his interest in art was first declared in 1874, with purchases of chromolithographs for the decoration of his house. A copy of Raphael's "Madonna of the Chair," some "fruit pieces" and genre paintings, and a portrait of Washington attributed to Rembrandt Peale were among the first oils he acquired.

In the next decade Oriental bronzes, etchings and engravings joined the growing number of paintings in his home, and by the time he decided to enlarge the original one-room gallery, he had further expressed his desire to share his art interest with others by establishing a gallery in the Minneapolis Public Library, supplying it with gifts and loans of pictures and objects of art.

By the turn of the century, when his collection numbered around 200 paintings and a thousand other works, T.B. Walker began assembling with great thoroughness what proved to be one of the finest collections of jade in the world. To house his acquisitions properly he commissioned the present museum structure; it opened as the Walker Gallery in 1927, a short time before its founder's death.

The paintings he bought for the gallery were the fashionable pictures of the era by such members of the Barbizon School as Théodore Rousseau, Charles-François Daubigny and Jean Baptiste Camille Corot, together with Salon paintings by Adolphe William Bouguereau, Jean François Millet and others. Selected examples of these 19th-century works and the few old masters are shown now on a rotating basis.

To maintain the museum, Walker left a fund, administered by the T. B. Walker Foundation, which continues to be the center's main source of income.

Below: THE BATTLE BETWEEN CARNIVAL AND LENT. Attributed to Pieter Brueghel the Younger (1564-1638). Oil on panel. The artist is best known for frightening character representations. *Walker Art Center.* Gilbert Walker Foundation Purchase.

Above: BLUE HORSES by Franz Marc (1880-1916). Oil. In this work the rhythmic freedom of the horses' forms, repeated in the landscape, and the expressive color reflect the revolutionary spirit of early 20th-century art. *Walker Art Center.*

Reorganization in 1940 changed the name from the Walker Gallery to the Walker Art Center, and the institution has lived up to its name with a variety of activities in the arts. The breadth and scale of the operations may be gauged by the action of the trustees of the T.B. Walker Foundation in granting $400,000 and the land for the Tyrone Guthrie Theater, built on the art center grounds.

In the permanent collection of the center are some of the landmark paintings and sculptures of the 20th century, acquired in the last quarter-century. The "Blue Horses," an oil by Franz Marc, is a much reproduced work of *Der Blaue Reiter* (The Blue Rider) movement of 1911-1912 in which Marc was a leading force. *Der Blaue Reiter* name, according to Wassily Kandinsky, another leader of the group, derived from the fact that Kandinsky and Marc "both loved blue, Marc — horses, I — riders. Thus the name arose itself." In this Marc work, the rhythmic freedom of the forms of the horses, repeated in the landscape, and the escape from conventional to expressive color, reflect the revolutionary spirit of early 20th-century art in which German expressionism was a vital element.

"Church of the Minorites," a painting by Lyonel Feininger, dated 1920; Joseph Stella's "American Landscape"; and the colorful abstraction by Stuart Davis called "Colonial Cubism,"painted in 1954, are among the contemporary works.

Of the older paintings in the collection, one of particular interest is "The Battle Between Carnival and Lent," a rough and ready scene of early 17th-century fun and games, which is fascinating. It is attributed to Pieter Brueghel the Younger, son of the great Flemish artist, and in any case, is regarded as a fine example of painting of the time.

With the impressive collection of sculpture as with paintings, the emphasis is on the contemporary. The art center's Lyndale Avenue facade, remodeled in 1940, is complemented by the eight-and-one-half-foot-high bronze "Prometheus Strangling the Vulture," created by Jacques Lipchitz between 1944 and 1953.

Chief among the contemporary pieces in the Sculpture Court is the large "Reclining Mother and Child" by Henry Moore, while one of the largest major acquisitions is the nine-foot-tall "Cubi IX" by David Smith, the seminal American sculptor who died in 1965. The angular blocks of welded stainless steel, burnished to apparent translucence, are stacked and balanced dynamically and improbably. The center also has sculptures by Raymond Duchamp-Villon, Jean Arp and Alberto Giacometti.

Despite the importance of its contemporary collection, the national and international reputation of the Walker Art Center has grown largely from the avant-garde exhibitions it has originated and circulated over the years. The sculpture of David Smith, painting constructions by George Ortman, the new art of Brazil, London, Argentina and the slashed canvases of Lucio Fontana and numerous shows on special themes have fully justified the center's reputation for excellence.

Walker Art Center: Minneapolis, Minnesota. Open Tuesday through Thursday, 10 a.m. to 10 p.m.; Friday and Saturday, 10 a.m. to 5 p.m.; Sunday, 12 p.m. to 6 p.m. Closed Monday.

V SOUTHWEST

EL PASO MUSEUM OF ART

The hope and the promise, followed by the deed of gift, literally created the El Paso Museum of Art, and demonstrated once more the beneficent cultural role of the Samuel H. Kress Foundation. As they have in other cities, the representatives of the foundation set standards that lifted the sights of the El Paso art community and urged its members to take the necessary action to become eligible for a Kress gift.

This might appear to have taken place overnight but it was in fact the fruit of years of preparation in which Robert E. McKee of El Paso, through his association with the Kress family and the foundation, worked patiently to establish a museum of art of stature and promise.

There had been a museum of sorts in El Paso, although it was relatively new. The home of Senator and Mrs. W. W. Turney was given to the City of El Paso in 1940 for use as a museum, but not until 1947 was it officially accorded that status and named The International Museum.

El Paso has long been aware of its triple heritage of Indian, Hispanic and Anglo-American cultural traditions in a region with more people who are Spanish-speaking than English-speaking and that also has a large Indian population. The intention to give expression to this inheritance through collections of archeological, historical and artistic objects was evident in The International Museum holdings, and its transformation into the El Paso Museum of Art has only strengthened the aim to establish it as one of the outstanding art museums of the Southwest.

In 1959, anticipating the Kress gift, the name of the institution was changed, and the citizens of El Paso voted a $750,000 bond issue to remodel the old building and add east and west wings for exhibition galleries, an auditorium, a classroom, offices and workrooms. The new museum building was opened in 1960.

The best of The International Museum collection, much that came out of the homes and offices of old El Paso, now may be seen in a permanent exhibit in the downstairs Heritage Gallery.

In the new west wing three galleries, prepared expressly for the Kress Collection when it was installed in 1961, divide those works into the Middle Ages, the Renaissance, and the Baroque and Rococo periods, ranging in time from the 13th to the 18th centuries.

The 59 paintings and sculptures of the Kress gift provide a capsule history of Western art in a progression of changes in media, techniques and subject matter, and some famous names are attached to certain pictures.

The oldest painting portrays the "Madonna and Child" on a large wood panel, nearly four feet high and two and one half feet wide, and is attributed to the School of Lucca, dated about 1200. It is thought to have been for some time on the altar of the Dalmatian Church of San Domenico in Zara, before entering a private collection from which it came to the Kress Collection in 1950.

A charming pair of panel paintings, each depicting three youthful angels playing musical instruments, their eyes raised in adoration as part of an altarpiece, are attributed to Giacomo Pacchiarotto. They appeal to modern taste with their varied and detailed textures of clothing, hair and background, as well as through the careful drawing that involved some curious and naive foreshortening.

One of the most prominent pictures is the tondo "Madonna and Child" from the studio of Sandro Botticelli, a composition that Bernard Berenson has called one of the artist's last monumental designs; the painting is thought to be by a follower of the master.

A six-by-four-foot canvas picturing Mars and Venus with the infant God of Love, called "The Education of Cupid," has an impressive provenance dating back to 1621. While in the past attributed to Titian, it is probably from his studio, reflecting some of his manner.

Other remarkable pieces are the "Portrait of a Young Man," attributed to Jacopo Robusti Tintoretto; the painting of "Berenice" by Bernardo Strozzi, portraying the wife of Ptolemy III about to cut off the lock of her hair (as a thank offering for her husband's safe return from war) that legend says the gods promptly set in the heavens as a constellation; and Antonio

130

Canaletto's "View of the Molo" in Venice, showing the Doges' Palace in the righthand quarter; and Sir Anthony van Dyck's brilliant "Portrait of a Lady" (p. 146) which came to the Kress Collection from the Prince of Liechtenstein in 1951.

Van Dyck (1599-1641) was born in Antwerp, entered a studio when he was 11 and was accepted in the painters' guild before he was 19. From 1617 to 1620 he was employed by Peter Paul Rubens. Arriving in London in 1632, he began an amazingly successful career which came to a climax when he was appointed "principalle Paynter in ordinary to their Majesties" and knighted. During his last years he frequently traveled between Antwerp, Paris and London. His foremost works are probably his portraits, in which his elegant style and refined color are especially impressive in the portrayal of women, as is apparent in the work in the El Paso collection.

As the El Paso Museum of Art continues to collect, it hopes to trace several trails through art: Mexican pre-Columbian to contemporary; United States from colony to nation; art of the Louisiana Purchase; decorative arts of the Western world; and contemporary Rio Grande art. Visitors may expect to find, in addition to the permanent collections, one or more temporary exhibitions of which there are some 15 to 20 annually.

El Paso Museum of Art: El Paso, Tex. Open Tues. through Sat., 10 a.m. to 5 p.m.; Sun., 1 p.m. to 5 p.m. Closed Thanksgiving and Christmas.

Below: SAINT JEROME AND SAINT FRANCIS by Jacopo del Sellaio (1442-1493). Wood panel. Sellaio's intricate background frames a scene characteristically peopled with saints. *El Paso Museum of Art.* Samuel H. Kress Collection.

Above: THE SAVIOR BLESSING by Carlo Crivelli (c. 1440-c 1493). Wood. Probably the center of a predella. *El Paso Museum of Art,* El Paso, Texas. Samuel H. Kress Collection.

Below: PORTRAIT OF A YOUNG MAN by Jacopo Robusti Tintoretto (1518-1594). Oil. Tintoretto was a Venetian master. *El Paso Museum of Art.* Samuel H. Kress Collection.

FORT WORTH
ART CENTER MUSEUM

Symbolic of the growth of American museums, early in 1967 the still small Fort Worth Art Center Museum, which had just restored the word "museum" to its name, stood face to face on television with the powers of London, New York and Los Angeles. In the world's first telstar-linked auction Fort Worth outbid all rivals for the $105,000 painting, "Femme Couchée Lisant" ("Reclining Woman Reading") by Pablo Picasso, sold to help in the restoration of Florence's flood-ravaged art treasures.

Picasso, who was born in Spain in 1881, is the phenomenon of 20th-century art — the most famous living artist, many believe the greatest of the century and certainly one of the most prolific. At 14 he was already the master of the realistic technique, subsequently working in a wide variety of styles and media. An epoch-making change in his work occurred between 1907 and 1909 when, with Georges Braque, he developed cubism from a study of Paul Cézanne combined with that of Negro sculpture and primitive art; but he later went on to other styles. No other artist of the School of Paris can rival the profound influence he has had on the whole course of modern art. Fort Worth is fortunate to have the large (51 1/8-by-76 3/4 inches) "Femme Couchée Lisant," done in 1960, as an example of his later work.

Founded in 1910 as the Fort Worth Museum of Art, with a one-room art gallery in the Carnegie Public Library, its sponsoring Fort Worth Art Association presented exhibitions, lectures, classes, theater and music performances, and began to acquire a permanent collection of art.

In 1938, when Fort Worth had more than doubled

Below: SWIMMING HOLE by Thomas Eakins (1884-1916). Oil. Eakins, in his passionate search for visual truth, paid assiduous attention to detail. He loved to paint people in action and in arrested motion, as in this fine figure study. *Fort Worth Art Center.*

132

in population, a new one-room gallery and classroom was dedicated in a new public library and by that time among the works of art acquired was one that continues to be an attraction, Thomas Eakins' 1833 painting of "The Swimming Hole." Purchased in 1925, it depicts half a dozen nude youths sunning, swimming and diving from a rocky shelf on the shores of a quiet stream. It is a fine figure study as well as a reminder of past pleasure in rural America.

In 1946, by popular ballot, Fort Worth approved a bond issue for "an art museum" building. By 1950, still moving slowly, sale of the bonds was approved, plans for construction were made, and in 1954 the museum became a reality. Meanwhile, the concept of an art center led the art association to seek additional funds for a theater wing.

The benefactions of William Edrington Scott during his life, and after his death in 1961 through the William E. Scott Foundation, brought his modern art collection to the museum in 1963 and made the theater possible soon after. By 1967 the expensive Vollard suite of etchings had been acquired, followed by the telstar-auctioned Picasso painting, serving notice that the Fort Worth Art Center Museum would keep up its side of Amon Carter Square, where the new Kimbell Art Museum with its multi-million dollar collection will arise. These, with The Carter Museum of Western Art that recently acquired a large sculpture by Henry Moore for its front lawn, will give Fort Worth a triumvirate of active art museums.

Among the paintings in the permanent collection of the Art Center Museum is Rembrandt Peale's graceful portrait of "Rosalba Peale," dated 1846, which closely imitates "The Girl at a Window" by Rembrandt van Rijn, one of the pictures stolen from the Dullwich College Art Gallery in London on the last day of 1966 but recovered less than a week later. Rembrandt Peale, whose brother Raphaelle, also became a well-known artist, was one of the several children of the American painter Charles Willson Peale's first marriage, all of whom were named for artists. Perhaps it is poetic tribute that Rembrandt's namesake should appropriate the great master's composition.

Other works in the permanent collection include the likeness of 'The Countess of Egremont" by George Romney, a typical Jean Baptiste Camille Corot forest scene of about 1850 peopled with dancing nymphs, and the truly fine portrait of a child, "Jean with a Hoop," by Pierre Auguste Renoir.

While the collection ranges back to early Italian works, and prints and drawings of several periods number nearly 700, the main strength is in 19th- and 20th-century art, including selected works by Texas artists. A remarkable essay in paint called "Figures in

Above: ROSALBA PEALE by Rembrandt Peale (1778-1860). Oil. The painting imitates "The Girl at a Window" by Rembrandt van Rijn, for whom Peale was named. *Fort Worth Art Center.*

Space," by Arthur B. Davies, presents nudes floating, swimming, kneeling, standing, bowing and sitting in an ambiguous landscape amid which the figures flow and break like the waves of the sea.

The William Edrington Scott Collection brought the bulk of the modern paintings and sculptures into the museum. Scott assembled his contemporary works in the last 15 years of his life, beginning with Lyonel Feininger's abstract linear depiction of a steepled "Church on the Hill," a painting given to the art center during the donor's lifetime.

Like the man of independent decision that he was, Scott purchased works of art with scant attention to current fashions, unless to defy them, and as a result, the Scott Collection has character that is rare among small privately formed modern art collections. Merged with other examples in the Art Center Museum galleries, it seems inevitable that the less prominent artists' pictures will be played down in the effort to be *au courant*, but their presence will be felt.

Charles Umlauf's alabaster "Female Torso," the gouache "Quicksands" by Enrico d'Assia and Charles Rain's "House of Ghosts," both in the magic realist manner, and an abstract "Alder Gulch" by Cynthia Brants are all strong statements.

Among works by leading artists, Scott's taste for clarity and vigor is exemplified in Charles Sheeler's "Continuity" (p. 163), a painting in which the hard, precise forms of industrial architecture make a dynamically lyrical composition, and also in Reginald Marsh's oil, "Carousel," a Coney Island scene of a bare-shouldered girl with flowing hair under her broad-brimmed hat, seated like a princess, sidesaddle on the galloping wooden horse. Decisiveness characterizes the exotic "Yellow Cactus Flowers" by Georgia O'Keeffe, in which the petals have been painted with liquid contours and soft gradations of tone.

Other items in the Scott Collection which may

Above: YELLOW CACTUS FLOWERS by Georgia O'Keeffe (1887-   ). Decisiveness characterizes the exotic blooms in which the petals have been painted with liquid contours and soft gradations of tone. *Fort Worth Art Center.*

Right: FEMME COUCHÉE LISANT by Pablo Picasso (1881-   ). Oil. Purchased at first telstar-linked art auction. *Fort Worth Art Center.* Collection of the Fort Worth Art Association, purchased 1967: The Benjamin J. Tiller Memorial Trust.

help to indicate its breadth, are an Andrew Wyeth watercolor called "Prevailing Winds," which depicts a barn cupola with a pagoda roof and delicate iron weathervane; a watercolor of the sea by John Marin; Tom Benrimo's oil, "Reflections"; etchings by Picasso and James A. McNeill Whistler; tempera paintings by Morris Graves and Paul Cadmus; oils by Rufino Tamayo and Bernard Buffet; some old Japanese prints; and an ancient Greek icon — all parts of the Scott Collection, which may suggest the wide range of his interest.

Although by the standards of some museums the Fort Worth Art Center Museum collection is still small, the latest acquisitions are spectacular and imply that anything is possible. Old beside many of America's museums, slow to receive substantial civic support and to build up its holdings, the art center has always been active and now reaches for leadership.

Fort Worth Art Center: Fort Worth, Texas. Open Tues. through Sat., 10 a.m. to 5:30 p.m.; Sun., 1 p.m. to 5.30 p.m. Closed Christmas.

MARION KOOGLER McNAY ART INSTITUTE

The best known instance of an artist of talent who founded a notable museum undoubtedly is found in the origin of the Whitney Museum of American Art in New York. Gertrude Vanderbilt Whitney, a capable sculptor, was fortunate in having the means whereby the informal meetings of artists in her home grew into exhibitions and eventually into the museum of art that in 1966 moved into its new building designed by Marcel Breuer.

Similarly in San Antonio, the home of Marion Koogler McNay, where artists, students and visitors interested in art were always welcome, became a museum of modern art in 1954, four years after her death.

Her own fine collection formed the nucleus that has more than doubled since then through gifts and purchases. She too was an artist, born in Ohio, who studied in the School of the Art Institute of Chicago and made watercolor her métier.

When the famed Armory Show of 1913 moved from New York to Chicago, stirring up whirlwinds of controversy, it made such an impression on the young artist that she began intensive study of the new trends in art, and soon became an avid but discriminating collector.

Although the Armory Show contained much indifferent art, the leaders of the contemporary movements were represented and of these the expressionist painters made the strongest appeal to Mrs. McNay. Beginning with the major artists, her collection soon grew in depth with acquisition of works by Georges Seurat, Paul Cézanne and Paul Gauguin. The choice of paint-

Below: CHURCH OF ST. GEORGE DE DIDON by Maurice Utrillo (1883-1955). Gouache on paper. Utrillo generally used a rather conventional approach to his subjects, with fine color enhancing the lyric mood of his work. *Marion Koogler McNay Art Institute.*

ings by Chaim Soutine, Pablo Picasso, Amedeo Modigliani, Odilon Redon, Marc Chagall, Georges Braque, Jules Pascin, André Derain and Henri Matisse gave real stature to her assemblage of modern art.

One may speculate that the presence of so many impressionist pictures in The Art Institute of Chicago led Mrs. McNay to start her collecting with post-impressionism, but now the impressionists, too, are well represented in the museum by gifts, purchase and loans.

Her special interest in watercolors was expressed by acquiring examples of many European and American artists. Among the former are Pierre Bonnard, Heinrich Campendonk, Raoul Dufy, Picasso, Jean Louis Forain, Marcel Gromaire, Auguste Rodin, Tsugouharu Foujita, Paul Signac, Paul Klee and André Dunoyer de Segonzac, a very distinguished company. The American watercolorists are equally impressive, beginning with Winslow Homer, Maurice Prendergast, Mary Cassatt, Childe Hassam and Robert Henri.

Always interested in the creative artists, she sought out members of the group of New Yorkers who formed a colony at Santa Fe, New Mexico, becoming acquainted with John Sloan, B.J.O. Nordfeldt, George "Pop" Hart, Randall Davey and others. Sloan's fine 1928 "Self-Portrait" is in the McNay collection.

Of course there are watercolors by later Americans: John Marin, Charles Demuth, Lyonel Feininger, John Steuart Curry, Gifford Beal, Emil Armin and Thomas Hart Benton. Subsequently, the museum has added canvases by Marsden Hartley, Alfred H. Maurer, Arthur Dove, Max Weber and Andrew Wyeth. A special gift has made it possible to start a collection of the works of younger Texas artists.

The Southwest's influence led Mrs. McNay to take interest in the native Indian arts and crafts of New Mexico. Votive paintings and sculpture of the 1750 to 1850 era, including an impressive large crucifix, together with early Chimayo and Navajo rugs, jewelry and regional furniture, are in a special gallery.

In 1955, the year after the museum opened, came the first major and still the largest gift, the Oppenheimer Collection of around 200 examples of Gothic and medieval art. It comprises panel paintings, stone and wood sculpture, tapestries and decorative arts, occupying three galleries and the outdoor sculpture loggias. Included in the Oppenheimer gift were two impressionist canvases.

The striking influence of a museum on the cultural growth of a community may be illustrated by the bequest, received in 1965, from Mrs. John W. Todd, of a collection of 20th-century paintings and a group of fine prints, virtually all assembled after the opening of the McNay Art Institute with Mr. and Mrs. Todd as founding members of the Friends of the McNay.

Above: PORTRAIT OF THE ARTIST WITH THE IDOL by Paul Gauguin (1848-1903). Oil. The artist portrays himself in a quiet, reflective mood. *Marion Koogler McNay Art Institute.*

Any account of the important works in the museum must include Paul Gauguin's "Portrait of the Artist with the Idol," an oil painted about 1893, in which he portrays himself in a quiet and reflective mood. Gauguin (1848-1903) is one of the legends of art of the past century. A successful broker in Paris and spare-time painter with a family, he gave it all up at the age of 35 to devote himself to painting. A friend of Camille Pissarro, Edgar Degas, Vincent van Gogh and Cézanne and admirer of the impressionist style, he developed into one of the foremost post-impressionist painters. His use of large flat planes of color and concern for decorative patterns, which help to distinguish his work from that of the impressionists, began to be apparent in the paintings done in Brittany after 1886 and was

137

characteristic of the paintings completed in the South Seas after 1891.

Other particularly notable works in the museum are "The Portrait of Henri Gasquet" by Cézanne, "Christ and Disciple" by Georges Rouault and Picasso's "Guitar and Wine Glass," a collage of 1913.

The development of the art institute has required purchases of sculpture, ranging from five bronze studies for Rodin's "Burghers of Calais" to a string construction by the contemporary American, Sue Fuller. The Print and Drawing Collection, established about 1960 and centering on 19th- and 20th-century graphics, contains many excellent prints, the Caribbean sketchbook of 200 drawings by Pascin and a rare book of sketches from about 1887 by a Kiowa Indian.

The art institute building continues to have the atmosphere of the home it once was, with antique French and Spanish furniture, Oriental rugs and decorative objects, some of which are part of the foundation now established for an Oriental collection.

The steady growth and fine quality of its acquisitions make the Marion Koogler McNay Art Institute one of the outstanding cultural assets of Texas, as well as one of the oldest.

Marion Koogler McNay Art Institute: San Antonio, Texas. Open Tues. thru Sat., 9 a.m. to 5 p.m.; Sun., 2 p.m. to 5 p.m. Closed Mon.

Below: HOUSES ON THE HILL by Paul Cézanne (1839-1906). Oil. The great post-impressionist painter's work strongly influenced 20th-century artists and earned him the title, "Father of Modern Painting." *Marion Koogler McNay Art Institute.*

Above: TWO GIRLS IN ARMCHAIR by Jules Pascin (1885-1930). Oil. Pascin, who also did many Biblical and mythological studies, is best noted for his delicate and sympathetic representations of female subjects. *Marion Koogler McNay Art Institute.*

MUSEUM OF NEW MEXICO

A vast and complex range of interests and institutions make up the Museum of New Mexico in Santa Fe. Occupying six buildings, the museum covers such subjects as Southwestern archeology and history, with a separate archeological research center, and Indian arts and crafts from the past 100 years. The museum complex also includes the Museum of International Folk Art and the Fine Arts Building, which is devoted primarily to the art of the Southwest.

Still another of the museum buildings, now in the second half of its fourth century, is the Palace of the Governors, the oldest continuously used public building in the nation, and perhaps the oldest European-built structure within the continental United States. Erected by the Spanish and very likely in use in 1610, the palace ceased being the state capitol in 1900 when a new capitol building was completed. In 1909 it became the first unit of the Museum of New Mexico and it now contains exhibits of the archeology and history of New Mexico and the Southwest.

The palace faces an equally ancient plaza, which was pictured during the 1880's by an anonymous artist working in the American primitive style. The painting (p. 146), which is now in the Fine Arts Building, depicts such typical Sunday afternoon activities as a band concert.

Behind the old palace in the Hall of the Modern Indian are ethnographic exhibits, with artifacts, models and full-scale replicas of Indian dwellings. Two miles south in Santa Fe stand the buildings housing the museum's archeological research and storage facilities, and the Museum of International Folk Art, in which examples from many parts of the world are displayed, emphasizing those with Spanish traditions and relations.

Founded by Florence Dibell Bartlett in 1953, who also created the International Folk Art Foundation, the Folk Art Museum belongs to the State of New Mexico which supports it with the aid of grants from the foundation. In addition to permanent exhibits, there are special temporary exhibitions from time to time in both the Hall of the Modern Indian and the Museum of International Folk Art.

It is the Folk Art Foundation that sponsors two exhibitions-on-wheels that circulate throughout New Mexico, the children's "museumobile" that visits the schools annually, and an exhibit for adults that is accompanied by a curator and is set up in public halls throughout the state.

Across Lincoln Avenue to the west of the Palace of the Governors is the Fine Arts Building where the work of New Mexican artists and others who have lived in the state may be found permanently displayed. At first dedicated to New Mexican art exclusively, the museum extended its range to include documentary art of the Southwest. Accordingly, the drawings and paintings of those artists who made the visual record of the early West form part of the collection; among these are George Catlin, Ralph A. Blakelock and Albert Bierstadt.

Although the first generation of artists came from Eastern studios to paint the West, others, like Charles M. Russell, "The Cowboy Artist," who has a small bronze in the collection, made the West their home. Contemporary artists shown include members of the artists' colony at Taos and Peter Hurd of Roswell.

Two New York artists who built homes near Santa Fe, Randall Davey and John Sloan (1871-1951), first arrived in 1919, fell in love with the country, and stayed

Above: DIEGUITO by Robert Henri (1865-1929). Oil. Henri felt that his art should reflect the artist's involvement with life and the legacy of his philosophy can be found in his acutely observant portraits. *Museum of New Mexico.*

Above: MUSIC IN THE PLAZA by John Sloan (1871-1951). Oil. A warm painting of the American scene. *Museum of New Mexico*

to paint it. Sloan returned every summer for 32 years, living first in a house on Calle Garcia and later building a home six miles out of town. Davey settled permanently in a canyon three miles from Santa Fe and both have works in the museum.

When Sloan first knew the Museum of New Mexico he wished that it had a few good pictures, for at that time the museum practiced on open-door policy for local artists that made it little more than a tourist trading post. Sloan was influenced by the liberal views of Robert Henri, like Sloan one of "The Eight" and represented in the collection. Henri visited Santa Fe several times, beginning in 1917, and advised Dr. Edgar L. Hewett, the ethnologist who was associated with the museum and who was instrumental in the encouragement of Indian painters.

Sloan's own concern for Indian arts led to increased interest in preserving the old and fostering contemporary Indian work of high quality, an interest now evidenced by the Indian Arts Fund Collection housed in the Fine Arts Building and consisting of painting, pottery and various crafts.

Other Santa Fe residents were allies of Sloan in gaining recognition for Indian art and artists. One was Witter Bynner who had formed an important collection of Chinese art and also one of Indian art. The other was Amelia Elizabeth White who helped to organize and finance a traveling show of Indian art for the museum circuit.

The aspirations of Sloan and the others for the museum were finally realized when, in 1949, high standards were established by the museum; and, as its collections formed, it joined the ranks of important regional art institutions.

Museum of New Mexico: Santa Fe, N. M. Open Mon. through Sat., 9 a.m. to 5 p.m.; Sun. and holidays, 2 p.m. to 5 p.m. Closed Mondays (Sept. 15 - May 15), Thanksgiving and Christmas.

PHILBROOK ART CENTER

Museums of art that grow from carefully nurtured seedlings, sometimes a small collection, sometimes a building, have the power to draw upon the artistic interest of their communities and to flower by attracting gifts of collections that together soon make them lively and important educational centers.

One of these is the Philbrook Art Center, situated in a 23-acre landscaped estate not far from the heart of Tulsa, Oklahoma. It was the magnificent residence of Mr. and Mrs. Waite Phillips until, beginning in 1938, the owners swiftly transformed it into an art museum and a center for activities in all the arts, broadly inter-

Below: MADONNA AND CHILD WITH THE INFANT SAINT JOHN. Umbrian School (16th century). Panel. Umbrian works are related to Sienese. *Philbrook Art Center.* Kress Collection.

preted to include art, literature, music and science, with special emphasis on preserving the records and encouraging the continuance of Indian arts of the region. The center opened in October 1939.

The arrival in 1953 of the Samuel H. Kress Collection of around 35 Italian paintings and sculptures of the 14th to the 18th centuries gave the art center new stature as the repository of the largest display of Renaissance art in that section of the country. Earlier, in 1947, the Laura A. Clubb Collection of more than 80 paintings, ranging from the 17th to the 20th centuries, added substantially to the museum's original holdings of pictorial art.

A collection of 54 watercolors and oil paintings was presented to the art center in the 1950's by the Standard Oil Company of New Jersey, and a number of special collections have greatly enlarged the founder-donor's initial gifts of native arts of the Southwest.

Throughout a large part of the museum building, which follows the style of a Florentine villa, the rooms, including the Great Hall with its Baroque pillars and beamed ceilings, the muraled Music Room, the Italian living room, the walnut-paneled library, and the dining room, have been maintained about as they were when the Phillipses lived in them, thereby continuing the gracious atmosphere of a palatial private residence as an aid to the art center's vital role in the cultural life of Tulsa.

The painting and sculpture in the Kress Collection serve as an enlightening background for native and contemporary American art, providing examples of European religious art, landscapes and portraits. The Kress pictures and sculptures include works attributed to Giovanni Bellini, Andrea Mantegna, Vittore Carpaccio, Annibale Carracci, Bernardo Bellotto, Lorenzo Ghiberti and Luca della Robbia (p. 164).

English, French and American paintings, particularly of the 19th century, may be found in the Clubb Collection, which must be rotated in its special gallery in order to leave rooms for the temporary exhibitions that enliven the museum's program.

Paintings from the art center acquisitions include serveral interesting works by Thomas Moran (1837-1926). Born in England and brought to America as a child, he was apprenticed to a Philadelphia wood engraver and learned to paint under the tutelage of his older brother Edward. At the age of 25 he returned to England and the impression made on him by the landscapes of J.M.W. Turner proved to be a lasting influence on his own work.

His landscape in the Philbrook Art Center, titled "The Spirit of the Indian," is one of the dramatic and romantic canvases produced as a result of his travels

(Continued on page 147)

Southwestern Museums

Left: Spanish Colonial Christo. New Mexico. This piece is unique in that the Santero, or saint maker, depicted the crucified Christ bent forward with arms flung back. On loan to the *Museum of New Mexico* by Bainbridge Bunting.

Below: ÉGLISE DE ST. BERNARD by Maurice Utrillo (1883-1955). Gouache. Utrillo is justly famous for achieving such personal and poetic studies of Paris and the French country villages that he loved. *The University of Arizona Art Gallery*. Edward Joseph Gallagher III Memorial Collection.

Above: PRAIRIE FIRE by F. Blackbear Bosin (1921-   ). Watercolor. Opposed to most symbolic and abstract two-dimensional Indian painting is this vivid and naturalistic scene of flight from impending disaster. *Philbrook Art Center.*

Right: THE GATE AND BEYOND by Peter Hurd (1904-   ). Tempera on wood. Hurd's love of his native Southwest and reverence for the plains combine in this realistic landscape which seems to suggest not merely a specific place, but a disappearing way of life. *Roswell Museum and Art Center.*

Right: BLUE MOON OVER THE STEEPLE by Alexander Calder (1898-   ). Calder gives us new concepts of weight and space in his light, free form mobile and stabile constructions. *The University of Arizona Art Gallery*. Edward Joseph Gallagher, Sr., Ann Hay Gallagher and Edward Joseph Gallagher III Collection.

Right: PORTRAIT OF A LADY by Sir Anthony van Dyck (1599-1641). Oil. This Flemish master of Baroque composition and portraiture was a favorite protegé of Rubens who influenced his style. *El Paso Museum of Art,* El Paso, Texas. Samuel H. Kress Collection, 1951.

Below: AMERICAN PRIMITIVE. Anonymous. Oil. The painter of primitives is often a recorder of pleasant scenes and experiences as in this charming 19th-century view of the Santa Fe Plaza. *Museum of New Mexico.*

(Continued from page 142)

in the West. In it the gigantic figure of an Indian, high in the mountains like an American Zeus on Olympus, broods over a scene of towering rock spires, wooded slopes and water.

Among the museum acquisitions are Lyonel Feininger's "Dunes," and the painting of a bleak, eroded hillside, with the plow that may have caused the devastation in the foreground, called "Mother Earth Laid Bare," by Alexandre Hogue.

These selections from the permanent collections also must be rotated, since the art center's active exhibition season includes loan exhibits, local and regional one-man shows, the annual exhibition by Oklahoma artists and the unique annual jury show of painting and sculpture by Indian artists, one of the largest in the nation, to which hundreds of works are submitted each year by Indians of many regions.

The founder-donor's concern for preservation of the Southwest's inheritance of Indian art and artifacts is expressed by the galleries that occupy the entire lower

Above: MADONNA AND CHILD by Taddeo di Bartolo (1363-1436). Tempera. Representative of the Sienese School's medieval period. *Philbrook Art Center.* Samuel H. Kress Collection.

Above: A BISHOP SAINT BLESSING by Vittore Carpaccio. Oil on panel. The artist dealt with his subject's pictorial possibilities. *Philbrook Art Center.* Samuel H. Kress Collection.

147

level of the art center. The Philbrook owns about 300 American Indian paintings which are shown in rotation and augmented regularly by purchases from the annual May exhibit of Indian art. One of the most interesting of these works is F. Blackbear Bosin's "Prairie Fire" (p. 144) in the Indian Painting Gallery.

The Santa Fe Room, which is unchanged since the Phillipses used it as a club room, has in addition to Indian art objects a painting each by Frederic Remington and Charles M. Russell.

The Taos Room combines native Indian, Spanish colonial and pioneer settlers' influences in furnishings that reflect these sources. Nearby is the Indian Artifacts and Costumes Room, which has a large mural by the Cheyenne artist Archie Blackowl depicting a traditional Cheyenne burial.

Installed in cases in the Spiro Mound Room are objects on extended loan from the University of Tulsa, taken from the Spiro Mound which was built by some of the earliest inhabitants of southeastern Oklahoma. Rooms for the important Clark Field Collections of American Indian Basketry and of Southwestern Indian

Below: SPIRIT OF THE INDIAN by Thomas Moran (1837-1926). Oil. Moran was born in England and brought to America as a child, learning painting under the tutelage of his older brother. At 25 he returned to his home country and the impression made upon him by J. M. W. Turner's landscapes proved a lasting influence upon his work. This dramatic and romantic canvas, with its spiritlike figure of the Indian in a panoramic landscape, resulted from his travels in the West. *Philbrook Art Center.*

Pottery, display Mr. Field's original 1942 gift and the additions that he has made since.

Southwestern archeology and history are represented by a dioramic setting for ceramics and implements excavated and presented by Mr. and Mrs. T. J. Darby. Another room is devoted to Southwest architecture, running the interesting gamut from ancient cliff dwellings to modern skyscrapers.

The beginnings of the Philbrook Art Center go back to 1938 when the Southwestern Art Association was chartered to receive and develop the Phillips residence as an art museum. The Tulsa Art Association, which had been sponsoring art activities in Tulsa, subsequently merged its collections and funds with the new association. To sustain the fledgling cultural enterprise, the Phillipses endowed the art center with income-producing properties in Tulsa.

Tulsa thereby acquired a well-formed art institution only 32 years after Oklahoma became a state in the Union.

Philbrook Art Center: Tulsa, Okla. Open Tues. through Sat., 10 a.m. to 5 p.m.; Tues. evening, 7:30 p.m. to 9 p.m.; Sun., 1 p.m. to 5 p.m.

Below: THE CRUCIFIXION. Follower of Pietro Lorenzetti (14th century). The works of the Lorenzetti family carried Sienese realism to excess, yet retained traditional religious idealism. *Philbrook Art Center. Samuel H. Kress Collection.*

Below: THE VIRGIN AND CHILD by Pier Francesco Fiorentino (active c. 1470-1500). A Florentine work influenced by Fra Filippo Lippi. *Philbrook Art Center. Kress Collection.*

PHOENIX ART MUSEUM

One of the youngest, and certainly one of the fastest growing, of the nation's art institutions is the Phoenix Art Museum which opened in 1959. During its brief existence the museum has tripled its physical size, and the beginning collection worth a few thousands of dollars has increased, through many gifts and purchases of fine quality, to a value in excess of $6,000,000. One well may ask how this came about without a major donor and with significant civic support only in the last stages.

The climate for fine arts in Phoenix had been cultivated assiduously on a small scale for 40 years, ever since some members of the Phoenix Women's Club decided to help the local artists and took over the fine arts displays at the state fair. Yet the sudden growth of Phoenix in the 1950's was the stimulus that brought about the concentration of interests and energies necessary to found an art museum and, with generous help from donors, to open the new building in 1959.

Within a year the structure was seen to be too small. Popular interest led to the voting of a bond issue for a new wing, and in 1965 the enlarged museum was open, able to show to advantage the swiftly accumulated treasures.

What makes the Phoenix Art Museum a mecca for the tourist, student, scholar and art collector is the quality and the variety of the works of art that have been acquired. In the handsome galleries beside a central courtyard with fountain and pool are examples of painting, sculpture, graphic arts and decorative arts from many lands; European art from medieval to modern times, Oriental, Mexican and American art.

With no plan other than the assumption that the museum should meet general interests and needs in

Below: THE WAVE by Gustave Courbet (1819-1877). Oil. Although Courbet was representative of the realist school, his paintings reflect the heroic tone, the drama and the worship of nature which characterized romanticism. *Phoenix Art Museum*. Cates Fund.

Beinlich

Above: FLOWERS, ITALY, 1931 by Joseph Stella (1880-1946). Oil. Stella is probably best known for his many representations of the Brooklyn Bridge, but his later works tended towards romantic fantasy as in these dreamlike flowers. *Phoenix Art Museum.*

art, it was decided to minimize the emphasis on art of the West and on American art, because good collections in these fields existed nearby. Emphasis was centered on securing gifts of European art to meet an evident need.

But growing so rapidly defies planning, and so the Phoenix Museum has an impressive group of American paintings to complement the fine collections at the Arizona State University in nearby Tempe. While acquisition of European art proceeded according to plan and with spectacular success, unexpected major gifts of Oriental art occasioned unintended, but nonetheless welcome, expansion in that field. A gallery of Mexican painting and groups of full-scale and miniature period rooms bring additional dimensions to the museum.

By any standards the gifts and purchases of French art have been unusual in a period of high prices and slim pickings. Ranging over a period of 300 years, works by many of the best known artists are included, some of them drawings but many of them paintings.

While Jean Antoine Watteau is represented by a small red chalk drawing of a greyhound, there is an oil self-portrait and a wash drawing by Jean-Baptiste Greuze, plus two oils by François Boucher, one of which is a happy depiction of two cupids bearing garlands, grouped together in a pyramidal composition that restrains their lively gestures. Another fine painting is Eugène Delacroix's "Le Christ au Tombeau."

Gustave Courbet was a painter with a strong feeling for the substance of things, and in painting "The

152

Wave" in 1870, a few years before his death, he portrayed the weight of a solid wall of water as it lifted up to break on the stony shore. Wave upon wave behind it to the horizon, and the heavy sky that fills a good half of the canvas, contribute to the effect of a massive onslaught.

The Barbizon School of landscape painters is represented by works by Louis Eugène Boudin (p. 166), Jean Baptiste Camille Corot, Diaz de la Peña, Jules Dupré, Jean François Millet and Constant Troyon. Claude Monet's colorful painting called "Les Arceaux Fleuris, Giverny," in which the floral arches are reflected in altered hues among the lily pads on the pond, is dated sometime after 1883; Camille Pissarro's late landscape with a red-roofed cottage, "Paysage a Varengéville," was painted in 1899; while another artist associated with the impressionist movement, Pierre Auguste Renoir, is included with a small undated ten-by-ten-inch oil, "Roses and Landscape."

There are drawings by Mary Cassatt, the American who worked so long in France, by Charles Despiau, Edgar Degas, Odilon Redon, Jean Cocteau and others; there are oils by Pierre Bonnard, André Derain, Maurice Utrillo, Francis Picabia, Jacques Villon, Pablo Picasso, Edouard Vuillard, Suzanne Valadon, Georges Mathieu and many more of the 20th century. "La Muse du Poète Guillaume Apollinaire," an oil by Henri Rousseau dated 1909, is a curious union of figures in a landscape; the principal subject, a woman armed with parasol and bouquet of flowers, has an alter ego in a pale winged figure also bearing flowers who hovers above among the trees.

The brusquely executed casein painting by Marc Chagall presents "The Holy Family" with Christ held upright in the Virgin's lap by Joseph, while in the background are Chagall's characteristic flora and fauna, with the head of his ubiquitous goat in one corner.

Chagall (1889-   ) is almost unique among 20th-century artist in having no disciples or imitators. He has been called a surrealist because the whimsical figures in his topsy-turvy world seem to be out of a dream; he has been called a primitive because of the apparent naiveté of his pictures with their childlike ingenuousness and lack of conventional perspective; he has been called an expressionist because he seems to revel in feeling. Chagall himself rejects these labels. He can only be classified as part of the School of

Left: HOLY FAMILY, 1955-1956 by Marc Chagall (1889-   ). Casein. The childlike ingenuousness of the Holy Family may have been influenced by Chagall's early and deep religious orientation. *Phoenix Art Museum.* Harrington Collection.

153

Paris, which places him geographically, not stylistically. It is easier to speak of the influences upon him, all of which stem from his Russian-Jewish origins — fiddle-playing uncles, an eccentric grandfather, a vast body of colorful folklore and a love of learning based on the Bible. This last obviously leading to such pictures as "The Holy Family" in the Phoenix collection.

Sculpture is highlighted by a small equestrian statue of Louis XIV by François Girardon; "Jaguar Devouring a Hare" by Antoine Louis Barye, the great sculptor of animals; "Genie de la Terre" by Jean-Baptiste Carpeaux; a version of Rodin's famed work "The Kiss"; a standing nude by Aristide Maillol; and two contemporary pieces, Ossip Zadkine's abstract "Cellist" and Germaine Richier's human mask called "The Eagle." All are in bronze.

While French art has a large place by intent in the Phoenix Art Museum collection, an extent only hinted in the preceding paragraphs, other European schools of recent years are well represented. A bronze head of a girl, "Kitty with Curls," by Sir Jacob Ep-stein, and sculpture by the brothers Gio and Arnaldo Pomodoro; drawings by Augustus John, Ernst Kirchner, Oskar Kokoschka and others; watercolors and gouaches by Giorgio de Chirico, Graham Sutherland, Eugène Berman, James Ensor and Gino Severini; a vigorous "Portrait of Count Basie" by Karel Appel, Massimo Campigli's grouping of doll-like figures called "Promenade à la Femme au Jaune" and oils by John Piper, Juan José Tharrats and Pierre Alechinsky, may suggest the nature of the contemporary collection.

Earlier works include "The Holy Family" by Sir Anthony van Dyck, and portraits by Sir Henry Raeburn, Sir Peter Lely and Nicolaes Eliasz. Picquenoy. José Clemente Orozco, Carlos Merida and Rufino Tamayo are chief among the group of modern Mexican painters while the highly presentable American collection starts with Washington Allston and John Singleton Copley and concludes with Alexander Calder and Andrew Wyeth. It does not neglect the abstract expressionists, is well supplied with examples of the Hudson River School, and shows a very strong hand in the 20th century with Marsden Hartley, Alfred H. Maurer, Milton Avery,

Right: LOUIS XIV by François Girardon (1628-1715). Bronze. This is a cast taken from a statue now in Paris. The original was destroyed during the Revolution. *Phoenix Art Museum.*

Below: PUTTI AND GARLANDS (Two Amorini) by François Boucher (1703-1770). Oil. Expressing gay Louis XIV style, this was probably overdoor decoration. *Phoenix Art Museum.*

Beinlich

154

Stuart Davis, Louise Nevelson, Isamu Noguchi and Max Weber.

Most of the artists are represented by single works but often they are strong ones such as Robert Henri's striking portrait called "The Laundress."

Among the windfall acquisitions, the Wong Collection of Ming and Ch'ing blue underglaze ware (p. 163) and the Luce Collection of older ceramics, constitute only a part of the Oriental art now assembled that includes Chinese paintings and sculpture from China and India.

Decorative arts have a particularly important place in a series of full-scale period rooms, together with the series of 16 miniature rooms created by Mrs. James Ward Thorne. These are 16 of the original 30 rooms prepared for the Chicago World's Fair of 1933-1934, and have been completely refurbished by Mrs. Thorne after their years of traveling in exhibitions.

Altogether this remarkable museum holds many pleasant surprises for the visitor. In a few short years the collections have become so excellent that other museums, including European institutions, now are borrowing for their special exhibitions.

Below: HOLY FAMILY WITH THE INFANT ST. JOHN by Marco di Antonio Palmezzano (1456-c. 1543). As a painter of the Umbrian School, Palmezzano displayed the Sienese sense of color and a deep feeling for beauty. *Phoenix Art Museum.*

Above: LA MUSE DU POÈTE GUILLAUME APOLLINAIRE by Henri Rousseau (1844-1910). Oil. In Rousseau's work ordinary people and forms become extraordinary and one finds the commonplace uncommonly revealed to the point where reality and unreality are closely joined. *Phoenix Art Museum.*

Phoenix Art Museum: Phoenix, Ariz. Open Tuesday through Saturday, 10 a.m. to 5 p.m.; Wed. until 9 p.m.; Sun., 1 p.m. to 5 p.m.

ROSWELL MUSEUM AND ART CENTER

There is something admirable about a museum that is wise enough and not afraid to collect and show the works of artists who live in its own environs, especially when so many American museums are going all out to educate the public in the art of the whole world and seek prestige by acquiring something, however slight, from the hand of every famous artist. Just as they lose their individuality by becoming similar, so the Roswell Museum achieves character by unique exhibits.

One of the New Mexican artists is Peter Hurd (1904-   ), who is represented by a special collection of his work. The original collection, donated in 1949, which has been augmented until it now numbers nearly 40 paintings in oil, tempera and watercolor, includes many ink-and-watercolor drawings and has a complete group of the graphic works of the artist. The collection

Below: IRIS by Henriette Wyeth (1907-   ). Oil. The artist sees the beauty and joy of the gifts of nature with a clarity that transcends their reality. *Roswell Museum and Art Center.*

continues to grow by addition of current productions and some from earlier years, and is intended to be a selected cross section of Hurd's art from the beginning.

After declaring his vocation by resigning his appointment at West Point in order to study with famed artist-illustrator N. C. Wyeth, Hurd found his way through studies at the Pennsylvania Academy of Fine Arts, followed by forming a strong affinity for the vision of George Inness. Searching for his own style, he began with oils, then oils painted thinly over gesso, followed by the classical technique of egg tempera on gesso. He next developed skill in watercolor as a *Life* Magazine war correspondent, and from this experience came the greatest freedom in evoking the space, clarity, precision of form and dramatic lighting of the West in both watercolor and tempera.

The range and strength of Peter Hurd's work, the sensitivity of his portraits, especially of women, and his ability to express the breadth and power of the land, as shown in his "The Gate Beyond" (p. 145), make the Hurd gallery a memorable experience.

The Southwestern Collection is devoted to artists who are natives or who have worked in the American Southwest, and presents paintings, sculpture, drawings, prints and crafts by contemporaries, including Henriette Wyeth who is married to Peter Hurd, Howard Cook, Robert Ray, Gustav Baumann and others. Many of them have been accorded one-man shows at the museum as part of its continuing program of temporary exhibitions.

Among the previous generations of artists are John Marin, Marsden Hartley and Georgia O'Keeffe; of the many, some are fugitives from Manhattan who found inspiration in the Southwest and created part of its cultural heritage.

Graphic arts provide the Roswell Museum with historic depth in European art from the 16th century. Rembrandt van Rijn and Pablo Picasso, Jacques Callot and Lyonel Feininger, Heinrich Aldegrever and Honoré Daumier, represent the art of four centuries in the various print media. There is, as well, a modest number of paintings by Americans not specifically related to the Southwest.

Perhaps the real surprise, coming as it were from a New Mexican source, is the Witter Bynner Chinese Collection, the gift in 1953 of the distinguished New Mexican poet. Over 200 examples of Chinese painting and work in jade and bronze, collected during his years in China, are rotated in a special gallery of Oriental style.

Witter Bynner, writing of his collection, noted that "Twice I happened to spend winter months at Peking; and each time toward New Year's, when all self-respecting Chinese are accustomed to start with a slate clean of debt, the best of the paintings came to me and were finally yielded, after days or even weeks of bargaining, at prices I could meet, some of them within the last few hours before the day of reckoning."

Founded in 1937 under the joint sponsorship of the Federal Arts Project, the City of Roswell, the Chaves County Archeological and Historical Society and the Roswell Friends of Art, the museum has enjoyed able leadership. It functions as a well-rounded art center with the usual activities while continuing to grow. In 1958 the physical plant was doubled in size by additions and more are planned.

While honoring its artists, the Roswell Museum and Art Center honors the pioneer rocket scientist, Robert Hutchings Goddard, often called the "Father of Modern Rocketry," who from 1930 to 1941 carried on his theoretical and experimental work near Roswell.

Roswell Museum and Art Center: Roswell, New Mexico. Open Monday through Saturday, 9 a.m. to 5 p.m.

Ken Corbean

Right: The Witter Bynner Collection of Chinese art was presented to the Roswell Museum in 1953 by the distinguished New Mexico poet. It includes over 200 scroll paintings and objects of jade and bronze which Mr. Bynner collected over a period of years. Exhibitions of the works are rotated.

Below: RAM'S SKULL WITH BROWN LEAVES by Georgia O'Keeffe (1887-   ). Oil. A distillation of images is achieved in the artist's studies of bones, a favorite subject of this fine American woman painter. *Roswell Museum and Art Center.*

THOMAS GILCREASE INSTITUTE OF AMERICAN HISTORY AND ART

In this day of multiplying and proliferating museums one often receives the impression that the goal of each is to be very much like all the rest in having a comprehensive collection and the means to survey the art of the entire world. Similarly, private collectors have shown a widespread tendency to acquire what can only be called fashionable collections, so much so that one contemporary collection is almost identical with another in the artists it represents.

A truly specialized museum, therefore, is a rarity, and while the scope of the Thomas Gilcrease Institute of American History and Art is certainly broad, in fact the Gilcrease Institute has displayed a primary interest in the history and art of the American West, and has collections of the work of artists who recorded the life and spirit of that part of the American scene. The institute also has an excellent library and a large archeological collection containing items from as long ago as approximately 20,000 years before the Spanish Conquest.

The Gilcrease Institute was founded by Thomas Gilcrease, who once said that "a man must leave some sort of track." Perhaps the principal reason he chose as his particular track the collection now housed in the institute was that he was one-sixteenth Creek Indian and extremely proud of the fact. In 1899 his father received 160-acre tracts of land for the Creek citizens of his family. In 1910, when he was 20, Thomas obtained drilling tools for his tract which lay in a region found to be rich with oil a few years before. He bought his first painting when he was 22; and by the time he was 35, his oil holdings had made him a wealthy man. In the following years he increased his purchase of those items that now make up the collection of the institute, now owned and operated by the City of Tulsa, Oklahoma.

From the extensive collection of the paintings and writings of George Catlin, who started up the Missouri in 1832, carrying his sketchbook, paint box and easel as part of his traveling gear, to the 1964 acquisition of the complete studio contents — pictures, sketches, models and equipment — of the contemporary painter of the West, William Robinson Leigh, the Gilcrease Institute has assembled notable and informative materials in which art is seen as the incomparable handmaiden of history.

Perhaps the best known of the artists is Frederic Remington (1861-1909), painter, draftsman, sculptor, illustrator, journalist and author of ten books. Of his approximately 3,000 oils, watercolors, drawings and bronzes, nearly all were of Western subjects and one of the largest collections is in the Gilcrease museum. The 26 paintings and 19 bronzes tell of the vigorous life of the plains in the last half of the 19th century. Although Remington was capable of quieter moods, as in a painting that records the appearance and traditional dress of Hopi Indian maidens, or in one that details an incident of camp life, the pictures and sculptures with the greatest impact are those that convey the hazards, battles and tragedies of the conflict between Indians and white men.

"The Coming and Going of the Pony Express," a vignette of the short-lived venture that carried the mail in relays from St. Joseph, Missouri, to Sacramento in eight days, is painted with dramatic emphasis as the rider dashes off on a fresh mount after a 15-second change of the mail pouches, while other men of the station rein the horse that has completed its 12-mile part of the run.

But Remington, who marched with the soldiers and won their respect, also knew and respected the Indians, and his paintings reflect the hard life and fierce struggles to the death of the frontier. From the discipline of drawing and painting in black and white for reproduc-

Below: RED JACKET by George Catlin (1796-1872). Oil. Catlin captured both the character and the pride of the Western Indian. *Thomas Gilcrease Institute,* Tulsa, Oklahoma.

Above: THE COMING AND GOING OF THE PONY EXPRESS by Frederic Remington (1861-1909). Oil. A vignette of the short-lived venture that carried mail from St. Joseph, Missouri, to Sacramento in eight days is painted with dramatic emphasis as the rider dashes off on his fresh mount after transferring mail pouches. *Thomas Gilcrease Institute,* Tulsa, Oklahoma.

tion, he developed a thin, dry, sensitive way with oil colors that caught the staring blue skies and harsh sunlight, the somber and brilliant hues of costumes, without sentiment and with authentic detail of form and action. His masterful understanding of the horse is displayed clearly in the bronze sculptures, also American classics, which some observers find better than the paintings, although Remington created only a few and made them late in his career, between 1895 and his death 14 years later in his native New York State.

George Catlin (1796-1872) was a successful portrait painter in the East when he began his Western sketches and paintings. The Gilcrease museum owns 75 oils, 137 watercolors, a unique book of his drawings and many letters, broadsides and books.

Catlin was on the Missouri a year before Prince Maximilian of Neuwied and the Swiss artist Karl Bodmer made their expedition to study and record the phenomena of the New World. His sketches provide invaluable documentation of details of Indian life, costume and implements, which he gathered in meticulous drawings for use later in paintings and lithographs.

In the Gilcrease museum may be found the largest known collections of work by two other artists who made their major reputations in the West, William de la Montagne Cary, who traveled up the Missouri in 1861, and Thomas Moran, whose greatest fame came from his

dramatic landscapes of the mountains and the Grand Canyon of the Yellowstone.

In 1871, Moran (1837-1926), English-born painter of the Hudson River School, accompanied an expedition into what later became Yellowstone National Park. Cramming his knapsack with sketches and watercolors, Moran prepared for the paintings that caused wonderment in New York and Washington a year later. Many of the watercolors are in the Gilcrease collection, and there is a portrait of Moran by William Merritt Chase.

Paintings and sculpture by Charles M. Russell, who was nearly as productive an artist as Remington, and works by Olaf Seltzer, Alfred Jacob Miller (p. 164), John James Audubon, Albert Bierstadt and others add to the pictorial heritage in the museum.

For anyone with specific interest in the varied, colorful, and largely vanished frontier life of the American West the Thomas Gilcrease Institute of American History and Art has much to reward a visit. In addition to its main field of interest, the institute has works by Thomas Eakins, Winslow Homer, James A. McNeill Whistler, John Singer Sargent, John Singleton Copley, Benjamin West and Gilbert Stuart, while collecting examples of contemporary Indian and Southwestern art.

Thomas Gilcrease Institute of American History and Art: Tulsa, Oklahoma. Open Monday through Friday, 10 a.m. to 5 p.m.; Saturday, Sunday and holidays, 1 p.m. to 5 p.m. Closed Christmas.

THE UNIVERSITY OF ARIZONA ART GALLERY

Modern Medicis seldom are unabetted, for their efforts attract the interest of others and soon there is united action. Nevertheless, in the beginning there may be only one, armed with initiative, and such a one was Dr. Richard A. Harvill, President of the University of Arizona, who welcomed the interest of the Samuel H. Kress Foundation from the start of his administration in 1951, and encouraged the development of wide-ranging collections for the university gallery.

Starting with the C. Leonard Pfeiffer Collection of American Art, with its special emphasis on the 20th century, Arizona gained a whole new world with the coming of the Kress pictures, since the foundation's concern has been Renaissance art.

Then the gifts of contemporary painting and sculpture from Edward Joseph Gallagher, Jr., provided the university with European and American art largely of the second quarter of the 20th century and later, to challenge both students and visitors with some controversial modern expression.

The Kress Collection, the first to be given to a regional museum, arrived in 1951 with an exhibition of 25 paintings, more than half of which remained in the gallery as the nucleus of the group of nearly 30 that includes a French 14th-century limestone statue of the "Madonna and Child," a gracefully poised figure with simple, flowing lines, that still retains traces of its original polychrome surface.

The earliest of the Italian paintings is a 14th-century 12¼-by-8¼-inch tempera on wood, a "Madonna and Child." It is thought to be by an unnamed Sienese artist, identified as the Master of the Ovile Madonna, after one of the most important of a group of paintings that seem to be by the same hand. The child-like pose of the Infant and the tender expression of the Madonna offset such primitive and archaic elements as the small head of the Christ Child and the diminutive hands of His Mother. An ornamental background of gold adds brilliance to the panel.

An interesting, and in Italy, extremely rare, example of a Custodia, with five hinged panels designed to close around the chalice with the Host, is painted with 16 scenes from the life of Christ on the side panels. The central panel is given to a single painting of the crucifixion. The artist who created these naively dramatic pictures is thought to have been a Florentine of the 14th century.

Paintings in the Kress Collection are attributed to numerous prominent artists, including Vittore Carpac-cio, Giovanni Battista Moroni, Jusepe de Ribera, Lucas Cranach the Elder and Giovanni Battista Tiepolo.

Unlike some of the Kress Collections elsewhere that extend only to the 18th century, the University of Arizona's pictures include a late 18th-century portrait of "The Countess of Schoenfeld" with her little daughter, by Marie Louise Elisabeth Vigée-Lebrun, who painted royalty in all the capitals of Europe, from Paris to St. Petersburg. In addition, there is a portrait group by Horace Vernet dated 1830.

One particular feature of the Kress gift is the 15th-century retablo of the Cathedral of Ciudad Rodrigo. The 26 large panels attributed to Fernando Gallego and assistants exemplify Hispano-Flemish painting of the time when these two poles of Europe were linked by many ties, including those of art. The eternal threat to art from war is illustrated by a large hole in one panel, made by a cannonball when the Duke of Wellington besieged the city during the Peninsular Wars.

Included in the Pfeiffer Collection is "The City" by Edward Hopper, painted in 1927. It is a clear view from an upper window, overlooking part of a square,

Below: CHRIST AND THE SAMARITAN WOMAN. Attributed to Fernando Gallego and assistants (15th century). Panel. *The University of Arizona Art Gallery.* Samuel H. Kress Collection.

Above: THE QUIET POND by Charles Burchfield (1893-1967). Watercolor. In his landscapes Burchfield sought the expression of a completely personal mood. *The University of Arizona Art Gallery.* C. Leonard Pfeiffer Collection of American Art.

with a colonnaded building that might be straight out of Paris in the foreground. A great block of monotonous "modern" flats of the early part of the century stretches out to the horizon. A watercolor by Charles Burchfield and Reginald Marsh's "Monday Night at the Metropolitan" are other Pfeiffer pictures.

The Edward Joseph Gallagher III Memorial Collection of paintings and sculpture is a large and remarkable assemblage of works reflecting a personal taste at once adventurous and conservative, very sound and yet not without sentiment.

Merely to highlight the collection touches on many works, of which a few must serve to suggest the rest. Examples of abstract expressionism include a small "drip" painting by Jackson Pollock. One of the turning-point paintings is Willem de Kooning's "Woman — Ochre" (p. 165), which is of the sort that marked a return to the figure for the artist after the reign of abstract expressionism.

De Kooning became prominent as an abstract expressionist, a totally non-figurative movement. Yet by 1950 he began painting several canvases of the image of a seated woman, all large and agitated. In this regard, de Kooning stated in 1951: "Art never seems to me peaceful or pure. I always seem to be wrapped in the melodrama of vulgarity."

The respectable French collection includes a 1954 wash drawing in ink, "Petit Clown à Cheval," by Pablo Picasso; the pen-and-ink line drawing, "Girl with Gold Necklace," by Henri Matisse; Fernand Leger's "Abstraction" in tempera and ink, and his gouache "Les Constructeurs"; the complexly patterned "Paysage Avec 4 Personnages" in gouache and collage by Jean Dubuffet; a charcoal drawing by Odilon Redon; Georges Mathieu's energetically brushed "Composition on Red"; the surrealist "Temps Egaux" by Yves Tanguy; and "Église de St. Bernard" (p. 143) by Maurice Utrillo.

Contemporary Japanese works in considerable number, and paintings by Europeans such as Karel Appel, Joan Miró, Emil Nolde and Karl Schmidt-Rottluff, plus an example of "op" art by the Israeli, Jacob Gipstein Agam, add to variety in the collection.

The American scene in art may be conveyed by a richly stained canvas by Morris Louis, and oils by Theodoros Stamos, Mark Rothko (p.166), William Baziotes, John Hultberg, Franz Kline, Arshile Gorky and Grace Hartigan, standing in contrast to some fairly conventional figure and landscape paintings. Alexander Calder's free form mobile, "Blue Moon Over the Steeple" (p. 145), is a fine example of the work of an outstanding American innovator.

Perhaps the range of styles and taste in the collection may be suggested by comparison of the suave five-foot-tall exaltation of the feminine form in the abstract, called "La Venus de Meudon," by Jean Arp, with Milton Hebald's "Harvest," also bronze and five inches taller, which is a grotesquely romantic mother and child reaching for an apple on a branch from which the child also seems to fall.

Similar contrasts are frequent and extend to several paintings by the donor that range from a tourist sketch of "L'Arc de Triumphe" to a sophisticated primitive work that defies classification, "Goddess of the Heavens."

What has made The University of Arizona Art Gallery particularly lively in the 1960's is the program of first-rate temporary exhibitions that have been originated, including retrospectives for Edward Hopper, Walt Kuhn, Henry Moore, Charles Burchfield, John Marin and Winslow Homer, a show of American painting from 1765 to 1963 from Lawrence A. Fleischman's collections and a charming exhibit, "The Bird in Art."

The University of Arizona Art Gallery: Tucson, Arizona. Open Monday through Saturday, 10 a.m. to 5 p.m.; Sunday, 2 p.m. to 5 p.m. Closed Christmas and New Year's Day.

Below: MADONNA AND CHILD by the Master of the Ovile Madonna. Siena (14th century). Tempera on wood. This gracefully poised figure retains traces of its original polychrome surface. *The University of Arizona Art Gallery.* Samuel H. Kress Collection.

Southwestern Museums

Left: CONTINUITY by Charles Sheeler (1883-1965). Oil. Sheeler's paintings are cool, silent perspectives of contemporary life, intellectual abstract compositions on a world dominated by its technical complexities and the machinery of men. *Fort Worth Art Center.* William E. Scott Collection.

Below: Chinese Underglaze Porcelain. K'ang Hsi period (1622-1722) and Ch'ing Dynasty (Mid-17th century). In the background is a lady's short jacket of the Ch'ing Dynasty embroidered in satin and Peking stitch on silk damask. The heavily carved chest reputedly comes from the Yuen-Ming-Yuen Palace near Peking, capitol of the old empire. *Phoenix Art Museum.* Dr. and Mrs. Mathew I. Wong Collection.

Right: WOMAN-OCHRE by Willem de Kooning (1904-   ). Oil. De Kooning's abstract expressionist canvases are brilliant, violent and striking works. *The University of Arizona Art Gallery*. Edward Joseph Gallagher III Memorial Collection.

Left: MADONNA AND CHILD by Luca Della Robbia (c. 1400-c. 1482). Polychrome glazed terracotta tondo. The harmony of composition and beautiful profiles in Della Robbia's reliefs made this new art form known throughout the Renaissance world. *Phoenix Art Center*. Samuel H. Kress Collection.

Above: INDIAN PROCESSION IN HONOR OF CAPTAIN WILLIAM STEWART by Alfred Jacob Miller (1810-1874). Watercolor. Miller painted as 2,000 wild Snake Indians paraded for Stewart in 1837. *Thomas Gilcrease Institute of American History and Art*.

Above: GREEN ON BLUE by Mark Rothko (1903-   ). Oil. It is the physical act of painting which concerns the abstract expressionists, not the portrayal of a concrete message or of meaning as such. *The University of Arizona Art Gallery.* Edward Joseph Gallagher III Memorial Collection.

Below: VOILIERS AU PORT (SAILBOATS) by Louis Eugène Boudin (1824-1898). Oil. Boudin captures the breezy atmosphere of the French coast in his delicate mode. *Phoenix Art Museum.*

VI WEST

E. B. CROCKER ART GALLERY

The persistence of an eleemosynary ideal can be remarkable and finds an instance in the Crocker Art Gallery collections of Sacramento, California, an almost accidental gathering of paintings, drawings and prints that has grown by attracting civic support first, and later the gifts of collectors.

When Edwin B. Crocker of Sacramento closed his law offices and moved his family to Europe in 1870, he had taken the first step toward realization of his dream by arranging for the construction of a museum building to house the collection he intended to acquire. Certainly this was a remarkable initiative in the days when the far West was more concerned with economic and social development than with cultivating the arts.

Born in New York State in 1818 and at first a civil engineer working on such projects as the Albany-to-Buffalo railroad, E. B. Crocker soon moved west to South Bend, Indiana. There he studied law before continuing on to California's gold country and the law practice that brought him a fortune.

So active a participant in the hurly-burly of Western life can hardly have had more than a glimpse of the kind of museum he dreamed of founding, and Crocker was ill-prepared to make the purchases necessary for the first-class gallery of paintings that he planned to create. Arriving in Europe during the Franco-Prussian War, he was forced to restrict his movements to Germany, yet the arrival of American wealth bent on acquiring works of art brought him immediate access to all sorts of art, and most of the pictures he was offered carried the names of the foremost artists.

Inevitably, in buying over 700 paintings, Crocker acquired one of the largest collections of German art in America. No matter how many of these works were attributed to Raphael, Titian and Rembrandt van Rijn, it was also inevitable that amid so large a sampling there would be some interesting pieces by other artists of merit, along with some that would be considered great treasures nearly a century later.

Furthermore, the practice of requiring the purchase of portfolios of drawings and prints, with the paintings, brought him over 1,000 drawings and a great number of prints. It was a time when prints and drawings were not considered important. It was the prints and drawings, however, that first attracted world attention to the Crocker Art Gallery, when in the 1930's, they were brought out from vaults and drawers for study by scholars who discovered masterpieces among them.

If there is no painting by Rembrandt in the Crocker collection, there is a tiny 3⅞-by-3¼-inch drawing in which the vigorous line of Rembrandt's quill pen gives life to "Saint Peter Liberated by the Angel." Among other works at the Crocker are the "Head of a Bearded Man" by Peter Paul Rubens, on buff paper in black chalk heightened with white; a pen drawing of a nude woman by Albrecht Dürer; a brilliant brush-and-bistre-wash drawing of "The Martyrdom of St. Sebastian" by Jacques Callot; "The Birth of Venus" by François Boucher; and drawings by Jean Honoré Fragonard, Jacques Louis David, Hieronymus Bosch, Sir Anthony van Dyck, Jacob Jordaens and Jacob I. van Ruisdael.

Dürer's copper plate engraving of "St. George and the Dragon," bearing his monogram under date of 1508, which shows the armed knight mounted at the moment of his triumph, is a prize of the print collection.

Crocker was not quite so fortunate with the paintings. They proved too numerous for his new gallery; and as a result a large number still are in storage, yet many fine examples can be seen in the museum. The 15th-century Flemish panel painting of "St. Bernard of Clairvaux Receiving the Stigmata from the Virgin"; the lively "River Scene in Holland" attributed to Jan ("Velvet") Brueghel; a precise still life of fruit by the Dutch artist, Jan de Heem; and the delightful little 8-by-5¾-inch self-portrait by Anton Raphael Mengs, are some of the earlier works.

There is also on view a remarkable collection of works by Dutch and Flemish masters of the 17th century, such as Andries Both, Jan van Goyen, David Teniers the Younger, and Philip Wouwerman, in addition to those already listed.

Three California painters of the 19th century are well represented. In the six-by-ten-foot oil, "Grand Canyon of the Sierras-Yosemite," Thomas Hill is seen in his first period when his Hudson River School back-

Above: ST. GEORGE AND THE DRAGON I by Albrecht Dürer (1471-1528). Copper engraving. One of the few prints of this etching still in existence, this probably is a symbolic illustration for a prayerbook. *E. B. Crocker Art Gallery*, Sacramento, Calif.

Above: MARTYRDOM OF SAINT SEBASTIAN by Jacques Callot (1592-1635). Brush and bistre wash on white paper. Planes of space and large sky expanses fascinated Callot. An esteemed craftsman, he was one of the first French artists to realize that space could be achieved through flattened planes of light and dark masses. *E. B. Crocker Art Gallery*, Sacramento, California.

ground dominated; later a trip to France led him to emulate the less grandiose and more intimate manner of the Barbizon School. Another Californian was the genre painter of the early years, Charles Nahl, whose large canvas, "Sunday Morning in the Mines," is filled with action, horse-play and humorous incidents. The third, William Keith, was a landscapist whose study in England brought him into contact with the work of John Constable with salutary effects on his later pictures of California.

The Crocker painting collections of the 15th through the 19th centuries have been balanced by gifts of sculpture of all periods. At the time when Collis P. Huntington built his palatial structure in San Marino, California, to house his English Georgian paintings and the Huntington Library, when other wealthy collectors who had started later than E.B. Crocker were founding their museums, some collectors wishing to make their holdings public gave them to the Crocker Art Gallery.

After living to see his picture gallery filled with paintings and the decorative arts purchased by his wife and four daughters, the founder died in 1875. Ten years later Mrs. Crocker gave the museum building with the collections to the City of Sacramento, and the California Museum Association was created to administer and develop the gallery.

Mrs. J. Sloat Fassett, a daughter of the Crockers who, with her diplomat husband, spent years in the Orient, returned with Chinese jades, ivories, jewelry, and a large and famous group of Korean pottery which she bequeathed to the gallery to found its Oriental collection. An example of the decorative arts of European origin is a lapis lazuli-and-crystaline vase (p. 184) of subtle coloring, created in a wave pattern in 1908 by Gertrud and Otto Natzler of Austria.

After decades of slow growth in the 20th century, when the gallery's holdings were still being explored, a new era began in 1959 with the organization of the Crocker Art Gallery Association. Primarily interested in art of this century, the association's first major acquisition was a six-foot-high bronze figure, "Atlantide," by Ivan Mestrovic, purchased by public subscription.

Through gifts and purchases the Crocker Gallery now has begun to assemble a very presentable contemporary collection of paintings, sculpture, prints and ceramics, mainly from the last 20 years. Californians Elmer Bischoff, Ralph Du Casse and Howard Bradford are represented with characteristic works. Prints by Henri Matisse, Jules Pascin, Emil Nolde, Georges Rouault and Carl Hofer, with paintings by the Mexicans, Roberto Montenegro and Rufino Tamayo give an international flavor to recent acquisitions.

Tamayo (1899-   ) — one of the four most renowned modern Mexican artists, along with Diego Rivera, José Clemente Orozco and David Alfaro Siqueiros — has been influenced by his Indian heritage and pre-Columbian forms. The result, however, as seen in his "Laughing Woman" (p. 183), is an individual style that is colorful, exciting and devoid of the social propaganda of much modern Mexican painting.

E. B. Crocker Art Gallery: Sacramento, California. Open Tuesday through Sunday, 10 a.m. to 5 p.m.

HONOLULU ACADEMY OF ARTS

In nearly every art museum, art gallery and art institute across America there will be found a thriving educational program that may center on children in one locality, adults in another or more often on both young and old. The responsibility for education in art is taken very seriously, and nowhere more than at the Honolulu Academy of Arts, whose founders placed the word "Academy" in the name of the institution, not because it was to be an art school, but to emphasize its role as a source of knowledge and inspiration deriving from its fine collections.

The only art museum in the Pacific devoted to the full range of Oriental and Occidental arts, and able to document its theses with many fine examples, the academy, of course, is the center of art activities in Hawaii. Honolulu, its metropolis, is a complex blending of many nationalities and races from Europe, the Americas, Polynesia and Asia, with a correspondingly complex cultural inheritance.

In founding the Academy of Arts, Mrs. Charles Montague Cooke and her family, descendants of missionary teachers, explicitly dedicated the museum to education "that our children of many nationalities and races, born far from the centers of art, may receive an intimation of their own cultural legacy and wake to the ideals embodied in the arts of their neighbors, that they may grasp that composite heritage accumulating for the new generations of Hawaii."

The great building of the academy which opened to the public in 1927 occupies a full city block in downtown Honolulu and was designed by Bertram Grosvenor Goodhue, architect of the permanent buildings of the Panama Pacific Exposition at San Diego, the Nebraska State Capitol at Lincoln and the Rockefeller Memorial Chapel in Chicago. The architecture of the academy gives practical expression to the museum's equal stress on East and West by the arrangement of the galleries of Far Eastern art around the Chinese Courtyard, from which one may look into the Spanish Courtyard with its surrounding galleries devoted to Western art.

The original collections of art, the gift of Mrs. Cooke, have grown in such fashion that a balance has been maintained among examples of European, Far Eastern and Pacific Ocean art, illustrating world art in some historical depth. Particularly notable additions to

Right: WHEATFIELDS by Vincent van Gogh (1853-1890). Oil. A powerfully brushed, rhythmic portrayal of fields under the blazing sun. *Honolulu Academy of Arts*, Honolulu, Hawaii.

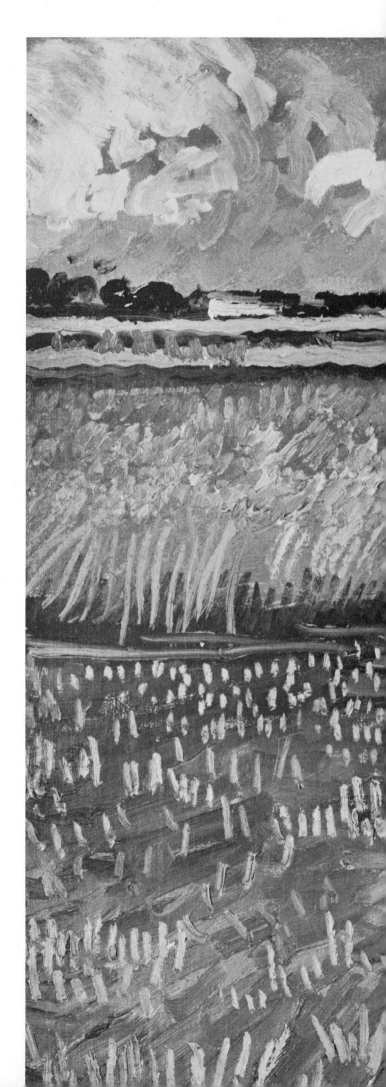

Above: Detail from FAIRY REALM OF ANCIENT JUNIPERS by Wên Chêng-ming (1470-1559). Ink on paper. This 12-foot scroll expresses the elaborate configurations of gnarled and twisted trees as if they were animate creatures. Wên Chêng-ming's broad, watery brushstroke technique reflects the tradition of past Chinese masters. *Honolulu Academy of Arts*, Honolulu, Hawaii.

Below: PLUM AND CAMELLIA BLOSSOMS by Kiitsu (1796-1856). To world art, Japanese painting contributed a splendid simplicity which focused on the essentials of its subject. Screens and wall paintings created to decorate the palaces of the nobility, depicted landscapes and blossoming trees with exquisite charm. *Honolulu Academy of Arts*, Honolulu, Hawaii.

the holdings of the academy have been made by Robert Allerton, who also made major contributions to The Art Institute of Chicago, and by the world-traveling author, James A. Michener, donor of an extensive collection of Japanese prints.

While contemporary art is well represented, including that of the Islands, the most famous work in the museum is "The Hundred Geese" scroll, an ink-and-brush drawing on paper usually attributed to the late 11th- or 12th-century master Ma Fên, but thought by some to date from a later period.

The geese in flight over marshland plants and water, or at rest on the still, reflecting water, are drawn with superlative skill and understanding. The Chinese painter rendered not just the birds' plumage and the characteristic patterns of flight, but interpreted the complex actions of turning in mid-air, landing on the water and taking off, all with perfect harmony of tone and spacing on the 15-foot-long scroll.

Another Chinese masterpiece is the 17th-century brush drawing called "The Coming of Autumn" by the Ch'ing Dynasty painter Hung-jên. This large scene of spare trees and great block-like cliffs and craggy mountains leads the viewer back and upward through a landscape in which the presence of man is discernible chiefly in a dwelling all but lost in the middle distance.

"The Fairy Realm of Ancient Junipers" is a scroll, 12 feet long by 11 5/8 inches high, that expresses the fantastic and elaborate configurations of the gnarled and twisted trees as if they were animate creatures. Dated 1532 and drawn in ink on paper by Wên Chêng-ming, whose life spanned the years 1470 to 1559 in the Ming Dynasty, this is another of the museum's great Oriental works.

The Chinese collection includes ancient bronze vessels, a group of 5th-century B.C. Hui Hsien tomb figures, and fine sculpture of which an important example is the serene "Bodhisattva Avalokitesvara" or "Kwan-yin." The latter is a seated figure, five feet, seven inches high, carved in well-preserved wood that once was polychrome and dates from about the 13th century.

In the Japanese galleries are a number of folding screens of special refinement and lovely, subtle color, such as the 17th-century two-fold screen attributed to Korin, with white chrysanthemums painted on a gold ground, and the six-part "Plum and Camellia Blossoms" screen by Kiitsu, a 19th-century painter.

Among the sculpture from Japan, the gracefully posed "Kichijo-ten" is a work of particular interest.

Below: Detail from THE HUNDRED GEESE. Attributed to Ma Fên, late 11th century or 12th century (possibly from later period). Ink on paper. The goose was much admired by the Chinese for his organization, leadership qualities and as a symbol of conjugal fidelity and the *Yang* principle, for as the goose followed the sun south in his migrations, so was a woman to follow her husband in all things. (See detail color illustration, page 183). *Honolulu Academy of Arts*, Honolulu, Hawaii.

This standing figure of a woman is carved in cypress wood and dates from the early 10th century.

Having all this in addition to the excellent Michener Collection of Japanese prints, and one of the world's most important collections of Korean ceramics, the Honolulu Academy of Arts is an exceptional treasure house of Oriental art.

Fine arts of the Western world are represented by ancient Greek and Roman sculpture and mosaic fragments, the Kress Collection of Renaissance paintings, and works by modern masters of the 19th and 20th centuries.

The academy received one of the largest of the Samuel H. Kress Foundation gifts, providing it with a group of panel paintings and canvases essential to the understanding of the development of European art between the 14th and the 18th centuries.

An outstanding work in the academy's collection is the "Adoration of the Magi" by the Flemish Master of 1518. Painted on wood, it is a rather open composition in which much is made of the richness of the attire of the three Kings and the details of architecture in the landscape seen through the arched entry to the scene of the Nativity.

The names Henri Matisse, Georges Braque, Pablo Picasso, Vincent van Gogh and Paul Gauguin are prominent in the academy's modern art galleries. One of the major works is a colorful 1890 painting by Gauguin, "Two Nudes on a Tahitian Beach" (p. 185). Vincent van Gogh's powerfully brushed oil, "Wheatfields," is a canvas such as he might have made outdoors under the blazing sun; shocks of wheat stand amid stubble in the foreground, and the flat fields extend to the horizon in a series of rhythmically related horizontal bands.

One of the famed late paintings of "Water Lilies" by Claude Monet gives representation to an impressionist painter, as Georges Braque's cubist still life, "La Pomme," illuminates one of the major movements of the 20th century.

Befitting a museum dedicated to educational aspects of art, the Honolulu Academy sponsors the annual "Artists of Hawaii Exhibition," as well as a program of major traveling shows that bring both historic and contemporary collections of the first rank to Hawaii. Among the Hawaiian artists whose work may be seen from time to time in the academy there are some native products of the academy's own Studio Program, others who have studied abroad and distinguished artists such as Jean Charlot, who has painted frescoes at the University of Hawaii, as well as members of the university's fine arts faculty.

Honolulu Academy of Arts: Honolulu, Hawaii. Open Tuesday through Saturday, 10 a.m. to 4:30 p.m.; Sunday, 2 p.m. to 5 p.m.

Far left: APSARAS. Japan, Fujiwara period (12th century). Gilded wood. In Hindu mythology, a supernatural female being who is mistress of a soul in paradise. *Honolulu Academy of Arts,* Honolulu, Hawaii.

Near left: ADORATION OF THE MAGI by the Flemish Master of 1518. Oil on Wood. Richly attired kings, detailed landscape and architecture adorn the Nativity scene. *Honolulu Academy of Arts,* Honolulu, Hawaii.

Below: WATER LILIES by Claude Monet (1840-1926). Oil. Monet's impressionist studies of water lilies provide an almost abstract vision of color, with a subtle Japanese influence. *Honolulu Academy of Arts.*

LA JOLLA MUSEUM OF ART

Above: BAGA NIMBA DANCE HEADDRESS. Guinea, Baga Tribe. *La Jolla Museum of Art.* Gift of Mr. and Mrs. E. B. Zeisler, 1961.

When the climate is propitious and the seed is planted in fertile ground, the tree will grow. The national climate for art was benign in 1940 when the first National Art Week was proclaimed and communities everywhere began preparing local exhibitions. La Jolla was one of them, for some of its artists undertook to organize a show.

With no place to hold the exhibit, some genie led them to the vacant former home of Ellen Browning Scripps, then up for sale, and there National Art Week was celebrated with community participation.

The climate was right, the seed was planted and the soil proved fertile. Leading citizens joined the artists to raise the funds to purchase the Scripps home, and in 1941, with minor remodeling, the Art Center in La Jolla was opened as a place for artists to exhibit throughout the year, and where educational activities in art could prosper.

In its setting just above the Pacific Ocean, the charm of the house and its outlook must have had much to do with making it a permanent center for art.

The tree grew. The bequest of Charles F. Meyer brought his art collection to the center and made possible the first major expansion in 1950, when the Meyer Gallery was added, together with classrooms and storage space. Ten years later the center was more than doubled in size through the bequest of Franklin P. Sherwood, acquiring additional galleries and classrooms, offices, an auditorium, landscaping and unification of the exterior by a modern colonnade.

In less than a quarter-century the art center grew from a one-time exhibition gallery to a museum, a development that was recognized in 1964 when the name was changed to La Jolla Museum of Art. Like other museums that have grown rapidly, gifts and the nature of what was available determined its course.

In 1956 the gift of Berthe Morisot's "Portrait of a Young Girl," drawn with oil sticks and pastels on canvas in 1886, was the inspiration for the exhibition, "Great French Painting, 1870-1910," the first major presentation of its kind in the San Diego area, with fine examples of impressionist and post-impressionist painting coming from great museums and private collections from New York to California.

One of the 25th birthday exhibitions in 1966 brought 70 oils and watercolors by John Marin and Marsden Hartley to La Jolla. By this time the museum had charted a course for its impressive temporary loan exhibitions and for the growing permanent collection, emphasizing 20th-century art and its immediate ante-

cedents, but including prints of four centuries plus primitive art.

Around 200 paintings and sculptures are in the permanent collection, most of them contemporary American, but with some interesting companions. One of several 17th-century oils is the precisely detailed "Canal Landscape Near Amsterdam" by Jacobus Storck, with its careful record of architecture, vessels on the canal and life along the waterway.

A watercolor by Odilon Redon entitled "Portrait of a Young Girl" and a work by Ernst Kirchner, "Self-Portrait with Model" (p. 186), are among older European examples. Kirchner (1880-1938) was the initiator in 1905 of *Die Brücke* (The Bridge), in association with Fritz Bleyel, Karl Schmidt-Rottluff and Erich Heckel. With no program other than direct expression of the creative impulse, they were fired by the intensity of Vincent van Gogh's painting, were aware of post-impressionist color theory and had seen paintings by Georges Seurat and Paul Signac. To this Kirchner added the strong impress of African and South Seas' art. Paintings composed of large areas of brilliant color seemed barbaric and posterish to German eyes in 1906 when *Die Brücke*'s first exhibition scored a *succès de scandale*. Later, after contact with French fauve painting, their work became more complex and less brilliant. The group dissolved in 1913 but left an indelible mark on 20th-century art.

The mid-20th-century European painting, "Anathemes Pontificaux," by Georges Mathieu, is a characteristic explosive knot of lines in heavy paint on a plain field.

The American group reflects the collecting habits of La Jolla. These include a salutary interest in California artists, and a broad, rather than specialized, approach to the national scene. Accordingly there are paintings by I. Rice Pereira, Louis Eilshemius and Karl Knaths, while sculpture is represented by Abbott Pattison's "Family Group," a two-foot-high bronze abstraction called "Watcher VII" by George Baker and Peter Voulkos' large, complex assembly of cast bronze planes titled "Big Remington III."

The print collection at the museum may hold more surprises in the contemporary field than the paintings. Although it began with examples of European etching and engraving from the 17th, 18th and 19th centuries, and acquired some good Japanese woodblock color prints of the 17th and 18th centuries, the gift in 1964 of the Mr. and Mrs. Martin Gleich Collection of lithographs brought a very special group of over 400 avant-garde works to the museum.

The lithographs, many of them in color, are the production of the Tamarind Lithography Workshop in Los Angeles, established with foundation support to provide working conditions and opportunities for artists similar to those of the print shops of Paris where Henri de Toulouse-Lautrec, Picasso and other great printmakers have worked. Some of the most prominent American and European artists have made limited-edition portfolios of lithographs at Tamarind. The artists include Josef Albers, Rico Lebrun, Louise Nevelson, Rufino Tamayo and some exponents of "pop" and "op" art, giving much variety to the collection.

Below: CANAL LANDSCAPE NEAR AMSTERDAM by Jacobus Storck (active c. 1660-1686). Oil. A precisely detailed 17th-century oil gives a careful record of architecture and life along the waterway. *La Jolla Museum of Art*. Gift of Mr. Ivan B. Hart.

Several hundred 20th-century prints in other media round out La Jolla's holdings among which are the two-part color etching, "My Son Leonardo," by the eminent American, Mauricio Lasansky and Georges Rouault's "Le Grande Pierrot," also a color etching.

Since 1960, a third field of museum concern has been primitive art. The gifts of Mrs. Lazzetta Gary initiated the African collection which now numbers some 150 works, specially installed under dramatic illumination. Oceanic carving, mainly from New Guinea, and pre-Columbian sculpture and artifacts from Mexico extend the range of the primitive acquisitions.

Although contemporary American art may seem the most promising field to cultivate as the La Jolla Museum of Art sets out to become "a museum of first rank and national importance," history suggests that the institution's ultimate character will be decided by the gifts and collections it receives and the developments that they make inevitable.

La Jolla Museum of Art: La Jolla, Calif. Open Tuesday through Sunday, 12:30 p.m. to 4:30 p.m.; Wednesday evening, 7 p.m. to 10 p.m

Above: PORTRAIT OF A YOUNG GIRL by Odilon Redon (1840-1916). Watercolor. Redon was associated with the symbolist movement, but remained an independent artistic force, his later works characterized by bright iridescent color. *La Jolla Museum of Art.* Gift of Mr. and Mrs. Kenneth R. Rearwin.

Below: ANETHEMES PONTIFICAUX by Georges Mathieu (1922-   ). Oil. A characteristic explosive knot of lines is laid in heavy paint on a plain field in this mid-20th-century European painting from the museum collection. *La Jolla Museum of Art.*

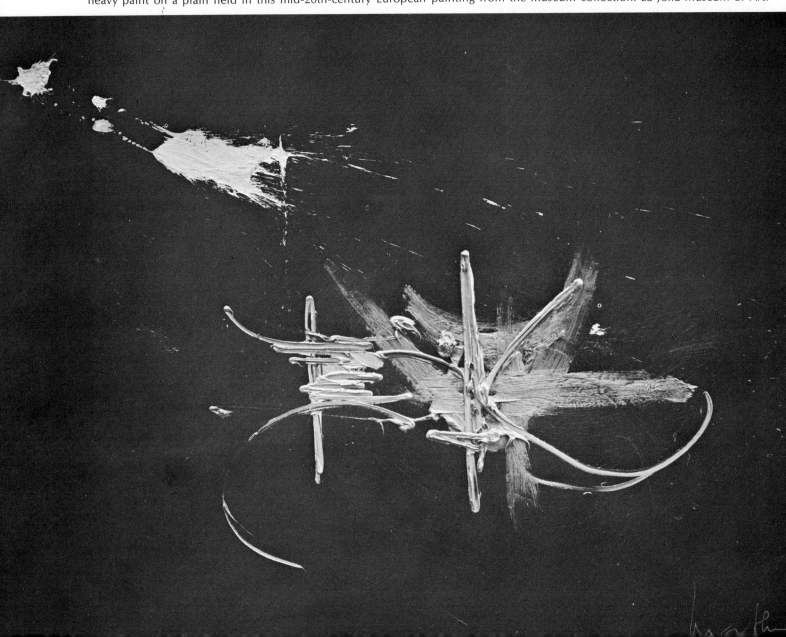

Above: LE GRAND PIERROT by Georges Rouault (1871-1958). Color etching. Rouault gave an almost mystical significance to clowns and thought they possessed the ideal way of life, but he generally painted them with tragic, time-etched or grotesque features, the color structure delineated by dark contours. *La Jolla Museum of Art.* Gift of Mrs. Pliny F. Munger.

THE PASADENA ART MUSEUM

One incontestable function of the big show, big name, exhibition program in a regional museum is to gain national status and thereby to stimulate local interest. In recent years the Pasadena Art Museum has mounted such a program with splendid results, crowned in 1967 when construction began on a new museum building in Carmelita Park at the western entrance to the city.

The museum's $6,200,000 program for development includes money for endowment as well as for physical plant that will nearly quadruple the size of the museum and increase fivefold the space available for exhibitions.

The new museum, with its sculpture court and sculpture gallery entrance, is so designed that rooms flow one into another. The curved corners of the H-shaped structure envelop and express the forms of galleries of varying height, size and shape, some with skylights, intended to display the permanent collections and temporary exhibitions under optimal conditions of space and light.

Although the print collection ranges over the centuries, with examples of the work of Albrecht Dürer, Rembrandt van Rijn, Francisco de Goya, Henri de Toulouse-Lautrec, Henri Matisse, Oskar Kokoschka, Pablo Picasso and others, the Pasadena Art Museum has concentrated on the 20th century and on post-World War II European and American art in particular.

A special pride of the museum is the Galka E. Scheyer Blue Four Collection, with works by Paul Klee, Lyonel Feininger, Wassily Kandinsky and Alexei von Jawlensky. The representations of Klee and Jawlensky have been considered the finest in the nation. Certainly the German expressionist movement in which they had a part has been one of the most influential sources in 20th-century art.

Paul Klee (1879-1940) was among the most original and inventive artists of the 20th century. His imagery, such as in "Maid of Saxony" (p.186) in the Pasadena Museum, seems to spring from a purely private source. Forms are treated in a visually unrealistic manner, but are seldom completely unrecognizable. His use of color is rich, varied and often bold, never descriptive. The charming and playfully profound results he achieved, were not purely intuitive, however, for he attached great importance to observation and technique and was deeply concerned with aesthetic theory.

The first part of this century is represented in the museum through paintings, drawings and sculpture by most of the well-known modern masters, including Picasso, Kurt Schwitters, Emil Nolde, Maurice Utrillo, Marcel Duchamp and Alexander Archipenko.

The "Head of a Young Girl" by Picasso (1881-   ) is one of a series of paintings done in 1928 in which the artist reorganized the human features with simplified, diagrammatic lines on flat grounds. In the Pasadena painting, the principal enclosed form scarcely resembles the head except for the fall of hair represented by six nearly parallel lines on the righthand side, and the proboscis at the top with two dots for nostrils. Mouth and teeth are indicated by the long stroke with short cross-lines, strangely oriented on a diagonal, more or less connecting two widely spaced eyes. While the painting is much more difficult to grasp alone than in the context of related works, it has the power to convey, in momentary flashes, the suggestion of a human face.

Schwitters' (1887-1948) collage of refuse, scraps of cloth and paper, cut, torn and pasted, called "Composition Black-Red" and dated 1921, was acquired through the Galka E. Scheyer Estate. Schwitters' collages, many of them tiny but carefully wrought, are little masterpieces in which texture, color and shape were the prime considerations in composition. The

Above: THE MAN IN THE TOMB by Oskar Kokoschka (1886-   ). Lithograph from "O. Ewigkeit Du Donnerworth." *The Pasadena Art Museum.* Gift of Mr. and Mrs. R. O'Neil.

Above: COMPOSITION BLACK-RED, 1921 by Kurt Schwitters (1887-1948). Collage. The artist's collages are generally composed of material he salvaged from the streets. He is representative of the post-World War I dadaist movement which declared its own war against the conventions and standards of society. *The Pasadena Art Museum.* Galka E. Scheyer Collection.

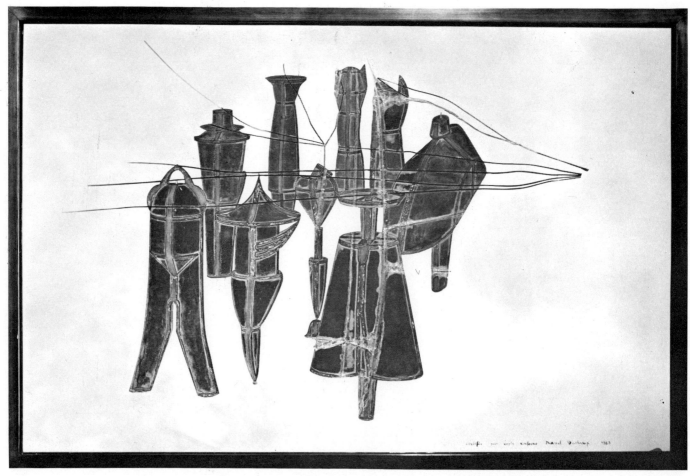

Above: NINE MALIC MOULDS by Marcel Duchamp (1887-   ). Painted glass, wire and sheet lead. Duchamp, also a dadaist, has had a penchant for using "found objects" in his works, which have been described as "anti-art." *The Pasadena Art Museum.*

lettering on tickets, labels and scraps of paper add humor, nostalgia or less pleasant overtones of meaning. Although Schwitters' work was valued very little during his lifetime, upon his death his studio collection was ardently sought after as collectors endeavored to add his special qualities to their holdings.

Under very able and ambitious directors, the Pasadena Art Museum has built a reputation for innovating exhibitions of contemporary art, as well as for shows of historical interest. A program of around 20 special exhibitions annually ensures constantly renewed opportunities for broadening artistic horizons.

While one of the special shows has been a national print competition, since discontinued, the unique contribution of the Pasadena Museum was to introduce in 1954 a series of California design exhibitions. Presented annually through 1962, this display of products designed in California was then rescheduled as a triennial, accompanied by a catalogue reproducing a permanent record of the best in California design of the preceeding three years. This program, supported by Los Angeles County, has made California design better known throughout the world.

The plan to use the old museum building as a Design Center after removal of other departments to the new Carmelita complex, is a further indication of the Pasadena Museum's interest in educating the public in good design and in helping California's artist-craftsmen.

The museum's special interest in contemporary art is expressed through its acquisition policies as well as in the temporary exhibitions. A major area of expansion of the permanent collection has been in the field of American art since 1945, during which time the works of such artists as Willem de Kooning, Sam Francis, Richard Diebenkorn and many others of the avant-garde have been acquired.

The new museum was planned with an Oriental garden and an Oriental art wing to house the large permanent collection of paintings and prints by such masters as Hiroshige, Hokusai and Harunobu, together with sculpture and ceramics from the Orient.

While incorporated in 1924 as the Pasadena Art Institute, supporters of the museum in 1922 had with great forethought made provision for future growth by purchasing the Carmelita Gardens site, where a new museum building was begun 45 years later.

(Continued on page 187)

Western Museums

Left: Detail from THE HUNDRED WILD GEESE. Attributed to Ma Fēn, late 11th century (possibly Ming Dynasty, 15th to 16th century). Ink on paper. In its entirety this work is generally considered to be the outstanding item in the museum's oriental collection. *Honolulu Academy of Arts.*

Below: LAUGHING WOMAN by Rufino Tamayo (1899-   ). Oil. Tamayo's work is derivative of pre-Columbian forms. *Crocker Art Gallery, Sacramento, California.* Gift of Crocker Art Gallery Association, 1964.

Above: HIS HEART SLEEPS by Charles Russell (1864-1926). Oil. Russell's solid paintings show an unusual scope, and are filled with the arid light of the prairies and plains. *Whitney Gallery of Western Art.*

Right: Vase by Gertrud and Otto Natzler. Austria. (1908). Spangled lapis lazuli and green crystalline glaze in a wave pattern. *Crocker Art Gallery, Sacramento, California. Gift of Mrs. Maude T. Pook.*

Below: TWO NUDES ON A TAHITIAN BEACH by Paul Gauguin (1848-1903). Oil. The French post-impressionist used exotic colors and simplicity of design to depict the gentle and unsophisticated lives of the Polynesians he lived among from 1895 to the year of his death, and left a major legacy to the new world of modern art. *Honolulu Academy of Arts.*

Right: MAID OF SAXONY by Paul Klee (1879-1940). Oil and encaustic on canvas mounted on mat with metal foil and gouache. Klee's playfully profound images became visual symbols of the German expressionist era. *The Pasadena Art Museum*. Galka E. Scheyer Collection.

Below: SELF-PORTRAIT WITH MODEL by Ernst Kirchner (1880-1938). Oil. Through a difficult life ran the thread of Kirchner's powerful expressionist imagination and his vivid emotional reactions to the world of the tragically real and the unreal. *La Jolla Museum of Art*.

(Continued from page 182)

From 1924 through 1942, the art institute carried on its exhibitions and other activities in Carmelita House, before moving into the former Grace Nicholson Galleries on North Los Robles Avenue, that served from 1943 to 1967. Although supported largely by private contributions, the museum was aided significantly by the City of Pasadena, not by bond issues but by special actions that amounted to public underwriting of the museum.

In 1941 the city took title to the Carmelita property with the understanding that if a museum were built there the title to the land would be retransferred. When in 1943 friends of the museum liquidated the mortgage on the Nicholson Galleries, they were deeded to the city which then leased the building to the museum at no cost. Furthermore, it was prearranged to allow purchase of the building by the museum so that it may serve in the future as the Design Center.

The name of the institution was changed in 1955 to the Pasadena Art Museum, and in 1966 the trustees announced a single gift of $1,592,000 from the H.C. Steele Foundation and Mrs. Jonathan Scott which, matched by gifts and pledges from the trustees and others, provided nearly half of the first phase capital needs of the art museum and permitted the initiation of construction.

The Pasadena Art Museum: Pasadena, Calif. Open Wed. through Sat., 10 a.m. to 5 p.m.; Tues., 10 a.m. to 9 p.m.; Sun., 2 p.m. to 5 p.m.

Below: HEAVY CIRCLES by Wassily Kandinsky (1866-1944). Oil. *The Pasadena Art Museum.* Galka E. Scheyer Blue Four Collection.

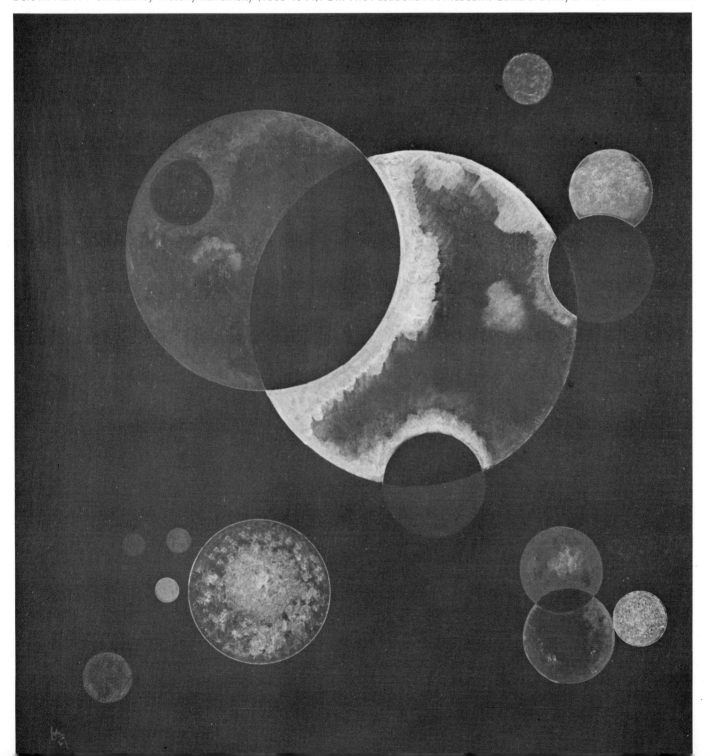

SANTA BARBARA MUSEUM OF ART

Fortunate is the community whose citizens have the interest, the knowledge and the means to acquire examples of the best in art. Santa Barbara is such a community, and so the Santa Barbara Museum of Art is able to follow a policy that emphasizes quality rather than quantity and that has brought into its collections many fine works and some that are truly outstanding.

Founded in 1941 in a centrally located building originally constructed as a post office, the museum, although standing on county-owned land, has been privately financed from the beginning.

About the time of the opening there was a new consciousness of the nation's artistic heritage, which was reflected in the Federal Art Projects and in the establishment of community art centers in many parts of the United States. Something of that spirit appears in the introduction to the catalogue of the museum's first exhibit, "Painting Today and Yesterday in the United States," which stated "Inasmuch as this new institution will function as a living art center in the community, as well as a true museum, nothing could be more fitting than making its initial presentation to the public the art of our own country."

From its opening the museum's public presentations included Greek and Roman sculpture on extended loan from the collection of Wright S. Ludington, a founder and continuous supporter, and the collection of American art that grew slowly, with principal strength in the post-World War I period.

Then in 1961 the Preston Morton Wing was added to house Mrs. Sterling Morton's 1960 gift of American paintings that about doubled the representation of the 18th and 19th centuries, completed the roster of "The Eight," and added other notable works from the first decades of the 20th century. The main gallery of the new wing holds the Preston Morton Collection of American painting, while the lower floor serves the many educational and community activities of an art center.

The small group of classical sculpture and Greek black-figured and red-figured vases occupy the Ludington Court in the center of the museum. With examples ranging from the 6th century B.C. to the 2nd century A.D., the sculpture collection includes a bearded male head, the earliest work, from the Island of Cyprus, and some fine Greco-Roman copies of Greek originals among which is the "Head of a Youth," thought to reflect the style of the 4th-century sculptor Skopas.

A playful "Satyr and Nymph" group, said to have come from Asia Minor, strongly conveys the sense of movement and counter movement, despite missing heads and right arms, as the nymph, caught by the Satyr's encircling arm, seems about to break away.

In two other galleries Oriental art is displayed, also primarily the fruit of collecting by the Ludington family.

Chief among the museum's European old master paintings are the predella panel of "Saint Ursula," attributed to Agnolo Gaddi; "The Holy Family" by

Below: HEAD OF A YOUTH. Unknown. Greece (4th or 3rd century B.C.). The museum contains some fine Greco-Roman copies of Greek originals, including this head in the style of 4th-century sculptor Skopas. *Santa Barbara Museum of Art.*

Above: BUFFALO HUNTER. Anonymous. America (c. 1830). Transcending the limits of naive style, this work combines a sense of the dramatic with an understanding of composition and design. *Santa Barbara Museum of Art.* Buell Hammett Memorial Collection.

Pieter de Witte, a Flemish interpretation of the Nativity from about 1500; and from the 17th century a three-quarter length figure of "A Franciscan Monk" contemplating a skull held in his cupped hands, painted by Francisco de Zurbarán.

Zurbarán (1598-1664), who today is recognized as one of the greatest Spanish painters, is perhaps best known for the haunting power with which he evokes mystical silence and solitude in such works as "A Franciscan Monk." He was influenced early by the Italian master, Caravaggio, who first brought a naturalistic style to religious painting and intensified his work with dramatic light and shade effects.

The museum's really excellent American painting collection presents a roster of the great and famous artists, yet has place for a fine Western primitive, the "Buffalo Hunter" by an unknown painter. Thought

to date from about 1830, in the picture the Indian hunter astride his handsome steed and aiming his full-drawn bow at the shoulder of the dark, plunging buffalo, is at the center of a tense composition of angular movement, set against the prairie horizon.

Before the arrival of the Preston Morton Collection, the Santa Barbara Museum's most important American paintings were two portraits by Gilbert Stuart, a Washington portrait attributed to Rembrandt Peale and several works by artists associated with the Hudson River School. The Morton Collection added distinguished portraits by John Singleton Copley, James Peale, Thomas Sully and Benjamin West to make a splendid representation of the early period.

Unlike some Western collections in which the works by Hudson River School artists suggest that the painters had changed allegiance to the Rio Grande, the Western

Above: STEAMING STREETS by George Bellows (1882-1925). Oil. The tempo of old New York is caught in Bellow's wintertime painting of a city crowd watching a man struggle with a team of rambunctious horses. *Santa Barbara Museum of Art.*

scene is not stressed at the Santa Barbara Museum. Paintings of the Yosemite by Albert Bierstadt and Thomas Moran, and California scenes by William Keith and Charles Nahl, are about all the museum has in this category until the 20th century when California artists painted the local landscape.

The museum has prime examples of *trompe l'oeil* still-life paintings by William M. Harnett and John F. Peto, while Eastern landscapes by Jasper Cropsey, Charles Codman, John F. Kensett, T. Worthington Whittredge and Alexander H. Wyant provide good examples of their art.

Thomas Cole, usually a painter of American landscape, here is revealed as the author of a classical invention called "The Greeks' Departure from Troy,"

reminiscent of Claude Lorrain. Works by four other American artists are the study of "Woman in Autumn Woods" by Winslow Homer, three landscapes by George Inness, a sensitive depiction of a boy in "Portrait of Master Alfred Douty" by Thomas Eakins, and Eastman Johnson's painting of a mother and children, "The Baby Carriage."

The Santa Barbara Museum also has characteristic pictures by "The Eight": Ernest Lawson, Robert Henri, Maurice Prendergast, Everett Shinn, William Glackens, Arthur B. Davies, George Luks and John Sloan. The tempo of the life of old New York is caught in George Bellow's wintertime painting of a city crowd watching a man struggle with a rambunctious team of horses. The picture, called "Streaming Streets," was painted in 1908, the year that "The Eight" rocked the art world with their seamy-side portrait of New York that brought them the unwanted name of Ashcan School.

Of course the Santa Barbara collection includes watercolors by John Marin, Charles Burchfield and Lyonel Feininger, oils by Marsden Hartley, Edward Hopper and a standard list of notables. In addition, it has works by important artists less routinely accepted in American collections, among them Alfred H. Maurer, Jerome Myers, Charles Demuth, Stanton Mac-Donald-Wright, Niles Spencer and Walt Kuhn.

The second quarter of the 20th century is substantially represented by the leading artists and a number of other works, some gathered through purchase prizes and gifts, to make a broader cross section than one finds in many museums. Santa Barbara's contemporary group continues the pattern of a not-too-stylish collection of avant-garde work, suggesting that the museum will maintain a comprehensive collection.

Although American art predominates, the great European moderns have not been neglected. An oil by Marc Chagall, "Young Girl in Pursuit," was given by Mme. Ganna Walska; among numerous Ludington gifts are drawings, of a ballet dancer by Edgar Degas, and of a peasant man and woman by Pablo Picasso. The small but growing collection of prints and drawings makes it possible to gather a wide range of artists.

Limited space requires that the permanent collection be rotated, and with around 30 temporary exhibitions annually, the museum presents a frequently changing face to the public. In addition, there are such unusual features as the Alice F. Schott Collection of historical dolls, the Henry Eichheim Collection of musical instruments, a collection of Russian icons, and one of ancient glass and gold coins.

Santa Barbara Museum of Art: Santa Barbara, Calif. Tues. through Sat., 11 a.m. to 5 p.m.; Sun., 12 p.m. to 5 p.m. Closed nat'l holidays.

Above: A FRANCISCAN MONK by Francisco de Zurbarán (1598-1664). Oil. The artist is best known for the power with which he evokes mystical solitude, using dramatic light and shade. *Santa Barbara Museum of Art.* Gift of Katherine Harvey, Wright Ludington, Mr. & Mrs. S. Morton, Mrs. E. L. Patterson.

WHITNEY GALLERY OF WESTERN ART

The Wild West lives on in art of many kinds — most recently, perhaps, in the popular arts through the television Western. The first portrait of the West, however, was modeled and painted before the turn of the century by a group of artists who traveled the trails and the uncharted prairie, who lived the rigorous life of the cowboys and soldiers, and who knew the Indians in the years when they still contested the encroachments of settlers on their hunting grounds. The portrait they left us has never been surpassed for authenticity and vitality.

Of one of these artists, Frederic Remington, his friend Theodore Roosevelt prophesied: "The soldier, the cowboy and the rancher, the Indian, the horses and the cattle of the plains, will live in his pictures and his bronzes, I verily believe, for all time."

Just outside Cody, Wyoming, associated with the Buffalo Bill Museum in the Buffalo Bill Historical Center, is the Gertrude Vanderbilt Whitney Gallery of Western Art, which opened in April 1959. Here are collected more than $3,000,000 worth of paintings, drawings and sculpture by artists who first placed on canvas the visual record of the West. Included are pictures once owned by Colonel William F. "Buffalo Bill" Cody, and portrayals of that colorful scout, soldier, rancher and showman; the contents of Frederic Remington's New Rochelle studio; and much other factual documentation of the winning of the West.

On the edge of the 40-acre Buffalo Bill Historical Center, placed where travelers, passing on their way to the nearby East Entrance to Yellowstone National Park can see it, is the heroic bronze equestrian statue of "Buffalo Bill the Scout," reining his mount and peering down as he signals direction with his upraised rifle. The sculptor was Gertrude Vanderbilt Whitney, in whose studio home the seeds of the Whitney Museum of American Art in New York were nurtured.

When William F. Cody died in 1917 at the age of 71, he had come a far journey from the Iowa log cabin in which he was born. Pony Express rider at 16, Civil War soldier, wilderness scout, ranch owner, founder of the town of Cody, his Buffalo Bill's Wild West Show toured the United States and Europe with a troupe of more than 500 Western cowboys and Indians, with horses and buffalos, to make him a living legend of the American West.

The Buffalo Bill Museum Association, founded in 1917 "to establish and maintain a Historical Center for the preservation of the History and Antiquities of the country," acquired a tract of land with the help of

Above: SELF-PORTRAIT by Charles M. Russell (1864-1926). Watercolor. A striking portrait of the self-taught painter and working cowhand. *Whitney Gallery of Western Art.*

Gertrude Vanderbilt Whitney and opened the Buffalo Bill Museum in 1927, furnishing it with innumerable memorabilia of the frontier.

Cody knew most of the Western artists and appreciated their work. His own collection of 31 oils and watercolors was sold to Mr. and Mrs. Pearl C. Newell with Cody's Irma Hotel to settle his estate. These works "came home" to the Whitney Gallery in 1964 as the bequest of Mrs. Newell who had resisted for 40 years all offers to purchase the pictures.

Important among the oil paintings is Rosa Bonheur's

equestrian portrait of Buffalo Bill, done in 1889 when Cody visited Paris with the Wild West Show. Other portraits of him, and scenes of the old West, make up the Cody Collection.

The Whitney Gallery, while stating that it is a gallery of documentary art and realistic pictorial records of the historic past, nonetheless is also a first-rate art museum because of the quality of its exhibits. It shows 72 paintings by George Catlin, made during his pioneer explorations up the Missouri River in 1832. These detailed visual descriptions of Indian civilization are from the Paul Mellon Collection, on indefinite loan from the National Gallery of Art.

Paintings by Alfred Jacob Miller (1810-1874), counted among artists of the Hudson River School, also focus on the life of the Indians. A pupil of Thomas Sully who later studied in Paris and Rome, Miller returned to Baltimore in 1834. Looking for some excitement, he moved to New Orleans three years later, working as a portrait painter, and there joined the expedition of Captain William Drummond Stewart which went west as far as Oregon. Recording the trip, Miller made many watercolor sketches of Indians and the mountains, the earliest pictures of the territory that now is Wyoming.

The Whitney Gallery also owns one of the largest and most important collections of paintings by another Hudson River School artist, Albert Bierstadt, whose spectacular canvases portray wilderness life and the magnificent Rocky Mountains landscapes.

Charles M. Russell (1864-1926), "The Cowboy Artist," was a self-taught painter and sculptor, and also a tough, rough working cowhand. The extensive collection of his work in the Whitney Gallery includes his striking "Self-Portrait," done at the age of 36. Russell's canvases and bronzes grew out of first hand experiences and many are filled with excitement and action, but he was also capable of quieter moods, as shown in his "His Heart Sleeps" (p. 184).

The artist to make the most complete record of life in the old West was Frederic Remington (1861-1909), who was born in Canton, New York. After study at Yale, where he played on Walter Camp's football team, Remington went west in 1880, traveling and living with Army troopers, cowboys and Indians to witness many of the scenes he depicted with such painstaking accuracy. What he could not witness, he re-created after thorough research.

His studio at New Rochelle was a veritable Western museum, for, in addition to paintings and sketches, it held an immense store of Western properties needed for his pictures: saddles, guns, articles of everyday Indian and ranch life, and memorabilia of his days on the frontier. Many are excellent and rare pieces.

After his death in 1909, paintings and bronzes and

Above: COLONEL WILLIAM F. "BUFFALO BILL" CODY by Rosa Bonheur (1822-1899). Oil. Painted when Cody's Wild West Show was in Paris. *Whitney Gallery of Western Art.*

his studio collection went to the City of Ogdensburg where he grew up, and there the large oils and sculptures were installed in an old mansion as the Remington Art Memorial. When in 1956 the trustees desperately needed to remodel the deteriorated building, they decided to part with the Remington Studio Collection which had never been put on exhibit. Acquired by the W. R. Coe Foundation, the Studio Collection, including 110 oil sketches, now is permanently reassembled in its entirety in a specially constructed wing of the Whitney Gallery of Western Art.

The attractive modern museum building, looking out past the Buffalo Bill statue to the mountains, provides a fine contemporary setting for the artistic heritage of the American West.

Whitney Gallery of Western Art: Cody, Wyoming. Open daily (May 1 to June 1), 8 a.m. to 5 p.m.; (June 1 to September 1), 7 a.m. to 10 p.m.; (to October 1), 8 a.m. to 5 p.m.

Index of Reproductions (Listed by artist)